30936

An Introduction to
CHURCH MUSIC

By

JOHN F. WILSON

MOODY PRESS

CHICAGO

Copyright ©, 1965, by

THE MOODY BIBLE INSTITUTE

OF CHICAGO

Library of Congress Catalog Card Number: 65-14612

Second Printing, 1967

Third Printing, 1968

Fourth Printing, 1971

Fifth Printing, 1972

Sixth Printing, 1973

Seventh Printing, 1974

Eighth Printing, 1975

Ninth Printing, 1976

ISBN: 0-8024-4133-5

To my wife June
and our children,
Karen, Cheryl, and John, Jr.

Printed in the United States of America

FOREWORD

In recent years, there have been significant changes in concepts regarding the ministry of music in our churches. On one hand, pastors and laymen have sought for a new and approved program to replace carelessly rendered musical offerings in their services. On the other hand, church musicians who have long advocated only the highest forms of music have begun to realize the value of worthy but simple materials designed to better communicate with people. The result has been a dual emphasis upon both quality and practicability, not only in music and texts but also in preparation prior to performance. The Bible-teaching church is now able to offer both spiritual food and aesthetic satisfaction to its congregation, and thus more adequately meet the needs of our present-day society.

With these changes has come a need for better understanding of the many aspects of church music as well as some uniform techniques for proper functioning. This book has been designed to assist many people, including the church musician, the participants in his musical groups, the clergy and the congregation. May the broad scope of the volume help each reader develop a fuller understanding of the overall ministry of music while stimulating him to further exploration into areas of particular interest.

The writer wishes to acknowledge those who read all or part of the manuscript and gave helpful advice, including Miss Blanche Branche, Mr. and Mrs. Virgil E. Smith, Kerchal Armstrong, Robert Carbaugh and Dr. Donald Hustad. Special thanks also go to Mrs. Myra Swanson and Mrs. Betty Harvey for the hours spent typing and preparing the manuscripts.

JOHN F. WILSON

CONTENTS

Chapter 1

CHURCH MUSIC - WHAT IT IS

Introduction

Church music is made up of many components. Even those people who are directly related to the field of church music, to say nothing of those who merely observe its operation, have diversified concepts as to what it is.

To the music publisher, church music is that which has been captured on the printed page, specifically designed for use in the church. It is cataloged in a category separate from "popular," "classical" and "school" music and is marketable only to certain musicians and dealers.

To the retail music supplier, church music consists of an array of equipment which includes pianos, organs, choir robes, batons, podiums and music library equipment.

To the professional musician, church music is one of the many phases of his art, directly opposite to secular music and usually restricted to certain types of literature, vocal and instrumental combinations, rhythmic, harmonic and melodic devices, all specifically suited to the church.

To the church musician, church music is a program of participation in choirs and other ensembles; an outlet for self-expression as a solo performer, director and accompanist; a means through which he can put his musical talents and training to good use; often a source of remuneration, and, more important, a means of serving his God and his church.

To the clergyman, church music is an aid to his own ministry in the church, as well as a source of wholesome activity and Christian ministry for many of his members.

To the member of the church board, church music constitutes a part of the many church functions requiring equipment, budget allotments, time schedules for the regular rehearsals and special programs, disbursement of salaries and remunerations, and general coordination with all the other departments of the church.

To the nonattending citizen of the community, church music is one of the symbols of the church life itself, an activity which may occasionally attract him to the church; a style of music associated with national disasters, special seasons, weddings and funerals.

To the member of the congregation, church music is an integral part of the church service, an activity in which the member, his children and other fellow laymen participate, and a source of personal inspiration.

Despite the fact that these statements are only generalities, they illustrate the many aspects of church music. To summarize, it is a musical style, an organization, equipment, an opportunity of participation, an expensive operation, a profession, a ministry, a source of attraction and a means of inspiration, all placed together to form a fascinating but complex form of art. In order to understand fully the functions of church music, one must learn to appreciate each one of these aspects and to see their values to the overall ministry of church music to the individual in the local church, on the foreign field, over the airwaves.

Before studying the distinctive characteristics of church music, we must first recognize the fact that it is *music*. Therefore it functions in the same manner as any other form of music and, to a certain point, obtains the same results. Music is defined as both a science and an art. Both science and art are involved in the composing, the performing, and the listening factors of music. Despite the fact that it is hard to determine just where one ends and the other begins, it is important to consider the contributing aspects of both.

Church Music a Science

A science is defined as a system; a classification of knowledge of many aspects of one subject. The scientific characteristics of music are identified by the musical symbols found on the printed page: notes, keys and clefs. However, the science of music is actually the construction and arrangement of the three main ingredients of music: melody, harmony and rhythm, systematically arranged into what is known as form. Each of these contributes to the sound which results when music is performed. More significantly, each plays a distinctive role in the overall effect which the music will have upon its listener. These components are defined as follows:

1. *The melody*—a source of identification. The melody is usually considered the basic thought around which the composition is built. To the listener, the sound is most often associated with the

identity of the composition, as well as being the easiest part to recall. Upon rehearing the melody, the listener is reminded of the title, text or mood of the piece. When hearing an unfamiliar work for the first time, his impressions are often based on his response to the melody. If it appears uninteresting to him, he loses interest in the rest of the music. If the melody speaks to him of joy, he will identify the music as joyful. Whether he finds the melody romantic, reverent, sensational or sensual will determine by and large his acceptance of the rest of the musical work.

2. *The harmony*—a projector of moods. Harmony is that combination of tones heard simultaneously, commonly referred to as chords. Although chords and chord progressions are not as easy as melodies to recall, they are even stronger projectors of moods and, upon being reheard, can often be identified by the kind of mood ideas they express. Because of the many different qualities found in chords and the many varied ways in which chords can be made to progress, it is possible for harmony to project countless degrees of expression, ranging from the very romantic to the ultra-dissonant. Because of this vast potential, harmony is at times capable of overpowering the mood expressed in its accompanying melody. Harmony also possesses the power of making weak melodies sound strong and causing strong melodies to appear weak.

3. *The rhythm*—the dominator of attention. Despite the strength of both the melody and the harmony, neither is as capable of stimulating attention and emotional responses as is this third ingredient. It is not only the most difficult component of music to define but also the hardest to control. In the hands of a careless performer, the simplest rhythms can overpower the mood ideas projected in the melody and harmony. On the other hand, a well-executed rhythm will greatly enhance the rest of the musical components. Rhythm can overpower the words in a song, or it can project them and give them greater clarity. Rhythm can cause both physical and mental discomfort to an individual, yet it is just as capable of being a source of tranquillity and repose.

4. *The form*—that which gives basic unity to the many ideas contained therein. The manner in which the melodic, harmonic and rhythmic devices are arranged and proportioned largely determines the extent of variety and contrast which will result when the music is performed. Good form is especially necessary when music is designed to project and interpret a text, such as in vocal and choral music. Even the hymn, which is usually written in one of the simplest forms, must be so constructed musically that the

melodic climaxes, harmonic resolutions and rhythmic accents all concur with the climactic phrases and word accents found in the text.
An outstanding illustration of compatibility between words and
music can be found in the hymn "Spirit of God, Descend upon My
Heart." In the accompanying example, the following points should
be noted:

a. The rhythm is virtually free from strong accents, syncopation
and rapidly changing note values. Such would be incongruous
with the attitude of quiet reverence suggested by the textual contents.

b. The pitch level of the melody coincides with the dynamic demands of the text. Note particularly the descending melodic line
accompanying the phrase "descend upon my heart" (See point *1*
in hymn), compared with the ascending notes found with "mighty
as Thou art" (point *2* in hymn), which build to the high point
(see *3* in hymn) in both melody and textual thought.

c. The harmony is conventional, and the voices move primarily
by steps, rather than in frequent and abrupt interval skips. All of
this contributes to the easy flowing movement which the text seems
to require.

An example of contrast to this hymn can be found in the gospel
song "Jesus Saves." The proclamation of this great message is found
in three of the four phrases (see point *1* in the hymn). Each time
the statement "Jesus saves" occurs, it is accompanied by a melody
which characterizes the proclamatory sound of a trumpet (point *2*
in hymn). The rhythm is of such a nature that it quickly attracts
attention, perhaps even startles the listener. The harmony remains
almost unchanging throughout, in this way contributing to the
stateliness of the hymn.

Church Music an Art

Although it is involved from the very beginning of the construction of a musical composition, the "art" aspect of music is realized
when the scientific formula of notes, keys and clefs is transmitted
into audible sounds by means of musical instruments and human
voices.

The performance of music is dependent upon the performer,
his instrument, his technical skill and his style of performance.

1. The performer—the executor of music. Needless to say, the
human agency is the most important factor in making music an
art. It is the performer who translates the symbols into sounds,
and it is to a large degree within his power to influence the ef-

Spirit of God, Descend upon My Heart

GEORGE CROLY

FREDERICK C. ATKINSON

1. Spir - it of God, de - scend up - on my heart;
2. Hast Thou not bid us love Thee, God and King?
3. Teach me to feel that Thou art al - ways nigh;
4. Teach me to love Thee as Thine an - gels love,

Wean it from earth, through all its puls - es move;
All, all Thine own, soul, heart and strength and mind;
Teach me the strug - gles of the soul to bear,
One ho - ly pas - sion fill - ing all my frame;

Stoop to my weak - ness, might - y as Thou art,
I see Thy cross— there teach my heart to cling:
To check the ris - ing doubt, the reb - el sigh;
The bap - tism of the heav'n - de - scend - ed Dove,

And make me love Thee as I ought to love.
O let me seek Thee, and O let me find.
Teach me the pa - tience of un - an - swered prayer.
My heart an al - tar, and Thy love the flame. A - MEN.

Jesus Saves

PRISCILLA J. OWENS   WM. J. KIRKPATRICK

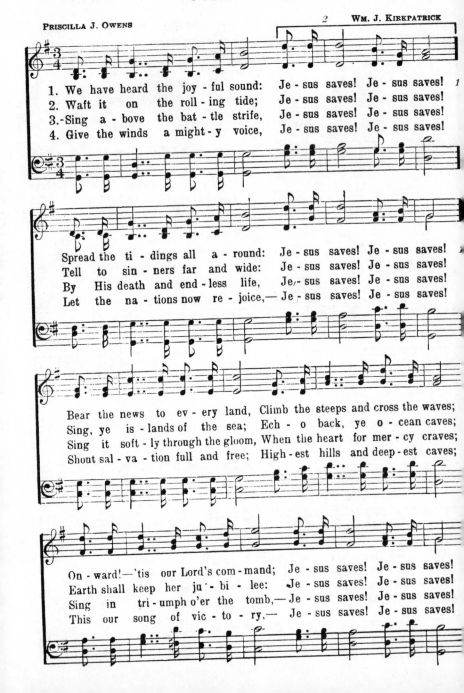

1. We have heard the joy - ful sound: Je - sus saves! Je - sus saves!
2. Waft it on the roll - ing tide; Je - sus saves! Je - sus saves!
3. Sing a - bove the bat - tle strife, Je - sus saves! Je - sus saves!
4. Give the winds a might - y voice, Je - sus saves! Je - sus saves!

Spread the ti - dings all a - round: Je - sus saves! Je - sus saves!
Tell to sin - ners far and wide: Je - sus saves! Je - sus saves!
By His death and end - less life, Je - sus saves! Je - sus saves!
Let the na - tions now re - joice,— Je - sus saves! Je - sus saves!

Bear the news to ev - ery land, Climb the steeps and cross the waves;
Sing, ye is - lands of the sea; Ech - o back, ye o - cean caves;
Sing it soft - ly through the gloom, When the heart for mer - cy craves;
Shout sal - va - tion full and free; High - est hills and deep - est caves;

On - ward!—'tis our Lord's com - mand; Je - sus saves! Je - sus saves!
Earth shall keep her ju - bi - lee: Je - sus saves! Je - sus saves!
Sing in tri - umph o'er the tomb,— Je - sus saves! Je - sus saves!
This our song of vic - to - ry,— Je - sus saves! Je - sus saves!

fectiveness of communication. His own efforts, personal attitude and native ability will all contribute to this. He is, however, not entirely responsible for this, as he is also dependent upon his instrument.

2. *The instrument*—the medium of execution. A performer is sometimes limited by the tool with which he must work, whether it be a small organ with only a few stop resources, a poorly maintained piano, a broken violin string, or an inadequate singing voice. While such impediments will place certain limitations upon the artist, they do not necessarily prevent him from giving at least an acceptable performance, especially when he possesses a good degree of skill.

3. *Technical skill*—the quality of execution. Even though it is important that the artist have an acceptable instrument, his technical abilities must be such that they can bring out the best qualities of that instrument, as well as meet the demands of the composition. However, a good musical performance is not determined by skill and musicianship alone but also by a good sense of expression.

4. *Style and expression*—the forces of communication. No performer is fully discharging his responsibilities as musical mediator until he has first captured the style of the composer and then expressed it clearly through the music. When this has taken place, communication is made possible. To assure the greatest degree of accomplishment, the performer must be putting forth his best efforts, the instrument must be in the best condition possible and his technical skill must be of the highest caliber possible.

Science plus Art a Means of Communication

It has been made quite obvious that the function of music is not complete without a third factor, the fulfillment of communication. As can be seen on the accompanying graph, there are three human agents involved: the composer, the performer and the listener, acting in three aesthetic agencies: the composition, the performance and the reception in bringing this fulfillment of communication to realization.

Science of Music	+	Art of Music	=	Fulfillment of Communication
Human agents		Composer	Performer	Listener
Aesthetic agencies		Composition	Performance	Reception

When music is performed, it is conveyed to the listener by means of two steps:

Perception—the stimulus of sound received by the ear.

Sensation—the transmitting of this sound stimulus to the mind.

These are immediately followed by a threefold reaction to the sensation, called response:

1. Mental response (understanding, wonderment, doubt)
2. Emotional response (joy, anger, fear, awe, contentment, grief)
3. Physical response (frowning, jumping, laughing, weeping, relaxing)

Although these responses will always occur in some manner, the nature of the response will vary greatly among individuals, as will the degree of satisfaction gained from one performance. At times the response will be quite contrary to that hoped for by the composer and the performer. This is usually caused by what is known as a breakdown in communication.

Causes for Breakdowns of Communication

To determine some of the many factors which may be involved in the breaking down of communication, it will be well to examine the composer, the performer and the listener in light of their responsibilities to the composition, its performance and its reception.

1. *The composer.* As creator of the music, the composer must assume full responsibility for his creation. Often a breakdown in communication can be traced to one of the following:

a. His poor choice or usage of melodies, harmonies and rhythms; a lack of good form; a weak text or an improper wedding of music and text.

b. His lack of knowledge or consideration of the limitations or potentials of the instrument for which he is writing, resulting in music which is either unduly awkward to perform or not designed to bring out the interesting characteristics of the tools used.

c. His failure to edit and notate the music carefully, making it difficult for the performer to fulfill the desires of the writer.

d. His lack of consideration for the listener's needs. The composer must write with sensitivity and imagination, and should know how to utilize the musical devices and dynamics which will assure the responses he desires.

2. *The performer.* When performing a musical work, an artist must accept the moral responsibility of executing it in a way in which it will best communicate to the particular listener for whom

he is performing. He may be guilty of breaking down the communicative powers through any of the following:

a. His failure to capture the thoughts of the composer. Although the performer is allowed certain liberties in his approach to expression, he should never do anything that would detract from the general nature of the piece, the climaxes and the contrasts of mood.

b. His inability to perform accurately. Before performing a work, the artist must evaluate his own musical capability and degree of preparedness in light of the work which he is to perform. One of the most frequent causes of breakdown of communication is a lack of mastery of notes, technique and facility.

c. His personal attitude toward the music. A prominent concert pianist once stated that she will never play any music which does not first bring true joy to her. Music must minister to the performer before it is capable of communicating a message to the listener.

d. His relationship to the listener. The media of communication must be readily accepted by the person to whom it is attempting to communicate. A performer will often fail to project the message of the music to the listener because of one or more distracting elements in his general appearance. A listener may develop prejudices against him because of such things as his apparent lack of good taste in clothing, his habits and affectations, or his physical appearance. As a result, there is no longer a willingness to respond favorably to his music. On the other hand, another listener may become so captivated by the performer's personal charm, appearance or physical endowment that his responses will be to the person rather than to that which is being performed. Again, the reputation of the performer or past experience of the listener with his performances can either be helpful or detrimental to the efforts of communication.

3. *The listener.* No doubt the most frequent causes of communication breakdowns are brought on by the listener. The prejudices and distractions previously mentioned are not entirely the responsibility of the performer, as they would have been nonexistent had they not been intentionally accepted by the listener himself. Two other causes are:

a. His unwillingness to accept unfamiliar music objectively. It is only natural that most people will enjoy music with which they are best acquainted. However, everyone should be willing to listen to and accept other less familiar styles and idioms even if he must do so with reservations at first.

b. His inability to understand the music. An open-minded approach to listening is the first and most important step toward overcoming this. As one seeks to develop good habits of listening, he will discover a great increase in the enjoyment he receives from music. As his knowledge increases, a greater desire for new sounds and styles will also be cultivated. Music which was once considered strange-sounding will eventually be accepted into the realm of the familiar. It should be remembered, however, that a musical composition does not need to be fully understood to be enjoyed, nor does the enjoyment of music need to be restricted to favorite styles or idioms.

It is conceivable that most listeners will favor the music which has always been considered familiar to them—that which they have heard and appreciated since childhood. On the other hand, they can also find that their newly acquired musical tastes will provide new joys and welcome variety to their listening experiences.

c. His inexperience as a listener. This factor is often detrimental to the listener's receptiveness to music. The skill of listening is one which must be developed through guidance, but more so through constant practice. There are three ways in which most people listen:

(1) Passively. Most people are accustomed to listening passively to the background music heard in a restaurant or department store.

(2) Emotionally. People are also usually able to recall at least a few instances when music brought about emotional responses, such as tears, joy, repose, reflection, or even fright.

(3) Intellectually. The most difficult method to develop is the intellectual, that which is employed by the scholar sitting in a lecture session. Intellectual listening helps one to understand and appreciate new things. In his *Introduction to Music*,[1] Hugh Miller suggests six prerequisites to the development of perceptive—or intellectual—listening:

(a) Attention, the putting aside of all other activities.

(b) Repetition, listening many times to the same thing.

(c) Familiarity, the by-product of repetitious listening.

(d) Background knowledge, the acquiring of general musical training as well as specific information concerning the music or style being listened to.

(e) Participation, humming or singing the themes while listening, then attempting to recall them at a later time.

---

[1] Hugh M. Miller, *Introduction to Music* (New York: Barnes and Noble, Inc., 1958), pp. 5-7.

(f) Auditory and visual approaches, studying the musical score while listening.

The most important function of music is its communication to the listener. According to Seashore this is fulfilled by "physical sounds (the composition), mediated through physiological organism (the performer), responded to by psychological organism (the sensation of the stimulus) in sensory experience (the response of the listener), and is reproduced and elaborated in memory, imagination, thought and emotional drives in their marvelous possibilities of intricate relationship."[2]

Music with a Spiritual Message

Music itself is not capable of making people Christians; neither can it cause them to worship. In fact, the major part of existing church music today is no different in style from that which is performed in other physical settings and for other purposes. The difference lies in its usage. While all music serves as a potent means of communicating and conveying a message, church music is performed for the express purpose of reaching people with a message from God. Its ministry is fulfilled when the performance is utilized by the Holy Spirit, thus becoming a vehicle of the great truth of salvation through Jesus Christ, which, when responded to by man, will result in making him a Christian. Likewise it is able to induce his worship of God. Therefore, the distinctive qualities of spiritual music are as follows:

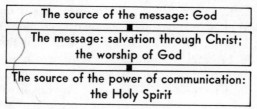

The source of the message: God

The message: salvation through Christ; the worship of God

The source of the power of communication: the Holy Spirit

Not all music performed in the church is effectively used of God. Some musical renditions contribute nothing more than atmosphere, others do little more than stir up emotions, while still others are of no value at all. There can be many reasons why this is true. The causes can often be traced back to the weaknesses of the composer, the performer and the listener in fulfilling their responsibilities, resulting in the breakdowns in communication previously discussed. On the other hand, the problems may

---

[2] Carl E. Seashore, *Psychology of Music* (New York: McGraw-Hill Book Co. Inc., 1938), p. 378.

be attributed in part to the physical environment: the temperature, architecture or other factors. However, assuming that the performer possesses adequate technical ability, the true source of the problem nearly always lies in the lack of spiritual force behind such performances.

Spiritual force is the divine empowering of the Holy Spirit which enables a composer to write that which can be spiritually effective when performed; a performer to yield his life and talents in a way that his presentation projects a spiritual message which can be understood by the listener; and a listener to be physically and mentally prepared to respond to the message presented to him. Spiritual force is an empowering which is far more essential than natural skills, understanding and inspiration.

It is not easy to discern between a message in music which is spiritually endowed and one which is not. Nor is it humanly possible to detect the time when the presentation of sacred music will be effective in communicating to man's heart and will, resulting in a conversion experience or an act of worship. It is only when the three—message, messenger and recipient—are united, prepared and used by God that one can be assured of either of these experiences taking place. It is therefore important that a careful analysis be made of these three factors to understand what is necessary in preparing them for effective use.

1. The music. The message of God can be conveyed through music in three different ways:

a. When the music embodies a sacred text (vocal music). In order that vocal music can be effectively used, there must be a prevailing union between the text and the music. When this is true, the music then becomes a transmitting force which is not only capable of interpreting but also of increasing the impact of the message contained in the words. However, this union will not be complete unless:

(1) The words are doctrinally sound and clearly written.

(2) The melody, harmony and rhythm of the music concur with the word accents, phrases and overall disposition of the text.

(3) The performance is a judicious interpretation of both text and music.

b. When the music suggests a sacred text (instrumental music). There can be much spiritual value gained in using an instrumental selection such as a hymn setting or choral prelude associated with a familiar text. Through the intellectual response of recall, those who know the text are able to meditate on the words or at least a few phrases and thus receive a portion of the message it contains. The effectiveness of this tool depends upon:

(1) The listener: who must be able to recall the words or general thought.

(2) The arrangement: which must project the correct mood idea of the text.

(3) The performance: which must be planned in a manner conducive to the text and music.

c. When the music helps to create an atmosphere for worship (neutral instrumental music). While a sacred text is the most direct way of presenting a message, it is possible to use neutral instrumental music to induce an attitude of worship when the following conditions prevail:

(1) The music portrays a definite spirit of praise, meditation, challenge or some other phase of worship.

(2) The worshiper has previously experienced a personal relationship with God and is able to maintain an inner worship experience himself.

It is also possible for neutral music to provide a setting which will increase the desire of the inexperienced worshiper to meet God and of the unconverted man to find the way of salvation. In so doing, it may establish in him a readiness of mind which will prepare him for a soul response to the message of the hymns, Scripture reading and sermon which follow. This is the greatest ministry music can render to one who has not yet responded to the message of salvation.

2. *The messenger.* The performer who desires to honor God and allow his talents to be empowered by the Holy Spirit is one who has experienced a personal commitment to God and is dedicated to a sacred ministry in music. Not all church musicians have this experience and desire. Some are using sacred music merely as a means of achieving secular goals.

There are two great distinctions between those desiring secular gains and those dedicated to a sacred ministry in music: the motives and their fulfillments. The following graph shows the general nature of the outlook of both types of musicians.

Both performers would no doubt begin with a motive clearly set as to whom they desired to serve: "Choose you this day whom ye will serve" (Joshua 24:15). Both will proceed to use the same medium, music. Both may even have the same degree of training

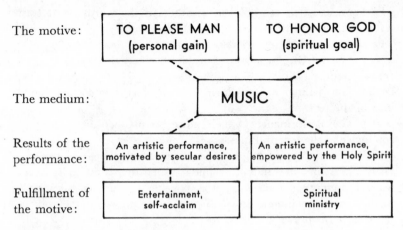

The motive: **TO PLEASE MAN** (personal gain)   **TO HONOR GOD** (spiritual goal)

The medium: **MUSIC**

Results of the performance: An artistic performance, motivated by secular desires   An artistic performance, empowered by the Holy Spirit

Fulfillment of the motive: Entertainment, self-acclaim   Spiritual ministry

and equipment. But differing motives will determine the manner of interpretation and presentation.

In both instances, the performance may result in an art, which is the aspect of music communicable to man; but the fulfillment of the motives will be different, because the motives themselves are directly opposite. The secular performer will have performed as unto men, while the sacred minister will have rendered service "in singleness of heart, as unto Christ; not with eyeservice, as menpleasers; but as the servants of Christ, doing the will of God from the heart" (Eph. 6:5, 6).

There are, however, other courses which are often taken by musicians, some legitimate and others perhaps out of ignorance or resulting from false motives. These courses include:

a. The use of music not necessarily associated with sacred texts to honor God. Some of these compositions, because of the nature of their style and structure, can be useful in honoring God. Though they must be carefully selected, many standard organ, piano and instrumental works serve well as preludes, offertories, and postludes, when neutral music is desired. The motive and the medium should be the same as when music with sacred associations is used. The results can also be spiritual and honoring to God.

b. The use of sacred music as an art. Often an oratorio, sacred solo, organ work or choral anthem will be used in a program designed strictly for artistic achievement, with no motive of honoring the God of whom this music was written. Such performances are not necessarily honoring to God. In fact, the music may be so beautifully rendered that a spiritual message will be conveyed to many who listen, but the main intention of the performer might be to please man or to receive personal acclaim for his accomplishments.

c. The use of sacred music as entertainment. In recent years there has been a noticeable trend toward using sacred songs in night clubs, television and other media of entertainment, often dressing them in a style that will identify them more closely with the popular ballads and "hit" tunes. It is unjust to condemn this practice as a whole, as there may be times when the performer's motive is to honor God and the setting such as would make it possible. Yet it is quite apparent that this is the exception rather than the rule.

d. The use of sacred music unartistically. There are times when sacred music is performed in such a way that it ceases being an art, especially when in the hands of the unmusical. The entertainment industry frequently condones this practice and even encourages it by paying huge salaries to untrained and unartistic performers. Their argument is that these performers communicate to those of below-average tastes. In the area of sacred music, it is possible that this kind of unartistic performance will be the result of the sincere attempt of an untrained person to honor God. In fact, it may perform a vital function in the local church and fulfill the ministry for which it is intended. For this reason, the performer should not be criticized, but rather encouraged to pursue further development of his skills. On the other hand, it is expected that his sincerity of purpose will result in an eventual improvement of his manner of musical expression, since it is virtually impossible to "grow in grace and in the knowledge of our Lord" without also growing and developing in all areas of one's Christian life. As the experience grows, so grows the expression.

e. The use of entertainment devices in a sacred ministry. It is true that church music itself is entertainment of a sort. As has been previously mentioned, sacred and secular music are closely related in style. There are, however, certain idioms and devices which are designed for entertainment alone. These should not be employed in sacred music, particularly in the church. While it would be impracticable to describe specific devices here, it is not difficult for one to discern between those which are acceptable and those which are not. The following five questions will help the dedicated musician determine the validity of certain questionable devices:

What is my motive in wanting to use them—to please man or to honor God?

Can I be certain that they will express the message of the text in the most convincing way possible?

Where did I first hear them used, and under what conditions?

Were the conditions comparable to those in which I will be using them?

Will my use of these devices serve as a reminder of secular things?

If all music were examined in this way, there would be little doubt that the devices used would be an honor to God and an enhancement to the music and the text.

In summary, the messenger must not only be dedicated to the ministry but also aware of the kind of music he should use, the manner in which he should interpret it and his motivations for using it.

3. *The recipient.* As has been noted, all music engenders three responses from the recipient: the mental, the emotional and the physical. There is still another response which comes as a result of sacred music: the response of the soul.

Psychologists differ widely in their viewpoints concerning the soul response. Some disclaim its importance by saying soul response is only another form of the emotions. Others believe it is the most inclusive of the responses, beginning with perception and functioning through the following:

a. The intellect: a mental response. (We think.)

b. The sensibility: a product of the emotions. (We feel.)

c. The will: a governor of the physical responses. (We desire to do.)

This theory is in keeping with the teachings of the Word of God concerning the soul. It is always referred to as the source of the affections, desires and active will. "Ye shall find rest unto your souls" (Matt. 11:29). "How long shall I take counsel in my soul, having sorrow in my heart daily?" (Ps. 13:2). Isaiah states simply, "Hear, and your soul shall live" (Isa. 55:3).

The recipient must, therefore, have a willingness to hear and to receive the message of the music before it will gain entrance into his heart. Based on Romans 10, the following outline shows how the message of salvation through Christ is conveyed through music, or any other form of ministry, to the ear, mind and soul of the recipient, thereby causing a response of the will. The Holy Spirit in turn empowers the messenger (Acts 1:8; 2:4), impresses the message upon the recipient (Acts 6:10) and causes him to submit his will to the message (Acts 8:6).

The Message

God, the source of the message: "Faith cometh by hearing, and hearing by the word of God" (Romans 10:17).
Christ, the fulfillment of the message: "Christ is the end of the law for righteousness to every one that believeth" (Romans 10:4).

The Media

Man, the tool of communication: "How shall they hear without a preacher? And how shall they preach, except they be sent?" (Romans 10:14c, 15a).
The ear, the avenue of perception: "How shall they believe in him of whom they have not heard?" (Romans 10:14b).

The Response

1. *The mental response, the intellectual understanding of the message:* "For they being ignorant of God's righteousness . . . have not submitted themselves unto the righteousness of God" (Romans 10:3).
2. *The emotional response, the heart acknowledgment of the message, and the desire to receive:* "How then shall they call on him in whom they have not believed?" (Romans 10:14a).
3. *The physical response, the active acceptance of the message:* "For whosoever shall call upon the name of the Lord shall be saved" (Romans 10:13).

RECOMMENDED READING

ASHTON, JOSEPH N. *Music in Worship.* Boston: Pilgrim Press, 1943.

BARTHOLOMEW, E. F. *Relation of Psychology to Music.* Rock Island: Augustana Book Concern, 1902.

BLACKWOOD, ANDREW W. *The Fine Art of Public Worship.* Nashville: Abingdon Press, 1934.

SEASHORE, CARL E. *The Psychology of Musical Talent.* Chicago: Silver, Burdett and Co., 1919.

———. *Psychology of Music.* New York: McGraw-Hill Book Co., Inc., 1938.

SNOWDEN, J. H. *The Psychology of Religion.* New York: Fleming H. Revell Co., 1916.

Chapter 2

MUSIC IN WORSHIP

Introduction

Worship is often misconstrued to be a routine of standing, sitting and kneeling at appointed times in an appointed place. Some people enter a service of worship having little or no concept of what they should gain spiritually from the experience. Although they often leave the service psychologically refreshed or emotionally stirred, they usually experience nothing of an act of worship. Still others consider worship to be an unnecessary distraction from the evangelistic ministry of the church, therefore they never take time to enter into this experience. Both types miss out on the true function of worship as Christ himself defined it: "They that worship him [God] must worship him in spirit and in truth" (John 4:24), and "Thou shalt worship the Lord thy God, and him only shalt thou serve" (Luke 4:8). Only as one fully understands the implications in these imperatives will he be able to fulfill the act of true worship of God.

Definition of Worship

Worship is a combination of an act and a discipline. The word itself comes from the Old English *weorthscipe,* meaning the ascription of worth. The act and discipline of worship involve two things which are essential to the experience:

1. Adoration. In England, *worship* is also used as a title of respect addressed to public officials. The ascribing of worth to God is, in a broad sense, an act of paying respect to Him; to praise Him for what He is and to meditate upon His greatness. Worship must then begin with an acknowledgment of God's supremacy. The end result of this should be the realization of man's insufficiencies in the light of God's greatness.

2. Submission. Even as one realizes God's supremacy and his own inadequacies, he must acknowledge God's sovereign rights upon his life. In so doing, he must dedicate his life to God. Wor-

ship is an act of submission to God's will. It is basic to the Christian's daily walk, and necessary to prepare him to serve, since it is the one act, following the initial experience of personal commitment, that brings God and man together in personal fellowship one with the other.

One of the greatest biblical examples of a complete experience of worship is found in the encounter Isaiah had following the death of King Uzziah (Isa. 6). After losing the one earthly idol which he had, Isaiah saw God "high and lifted up." Immediately upon seeing God, he realized his own uncleanness as well as the uncleanness of those around him. Upon acknowledgment of his sinfulness, his sins were purged (v. 7), the call of God was heard and Isaiah responded (v. 8). In this example it is evident that the call to service and evangelism is an integral part of the act of worship. One who desires to adore God must in turn submit himself for service. One who wishes to serve Him must first know how to adore Him.

Music in Biblical Worship

Ever since the institution of corporate worship, music has been its handmaid. Some of the outstanding biblical accounts of its use in public praise to God include:

1. The pilgrimage to the Promised Land. Moses and the children of Israel sang of their triumph over the Egyptians following the Red Sea experience (Exodus 15:1-21) and again when God provided water for them (Num. 21:17). At the climax of their journey, Moses gathered the people together to sing of the mercies of God, before going up into Mount Nebo to die (Deut. 32:1-43).

2. The establishing of worship in Jerusalem. At the time of the removal of the ark from the house of Obed-edom, David and all Israel played before the Lord on instruments (II Sam. 6:5). When the task was completed, a psalm of praise was sung (I Chron. 16:4-36). When the temple was dedicated, the praise through music was so greatly used that "the glory of the Lord . . . filled the house of God" (II Chron. 5:11-14).

3. The return to temple worship. When Hezekiah began his reign, he cleaned out the much neglected temple, established an orchestra and choir, and offered a burnt offering to the Lord while all the people worshiped (II Chron. 29:25-30).

4. The establishment of the new temple. Under the leadership of Ezra an orchestra and choir were reorganized from the returning remnant. Praises were offered to God while the foundation of

the temple was being laid (Ezra 3:10-13) and after the temple had been completed and dedicated (Ezra 7:7-10).

5. The Last Supper. On the final evening before Christ went out into the Mount of Olives, He and his disciples sang a hymn together (Matt. 26:26-30). This hymn is believed to have been the Hallel, a name associated with Psalms 113-118.

Music in Early Church Worship

The early Christian church followed many of the worship patterns established in the temple during the time of David. As the years progressed, the relevance of music in worship either increased or diminished according to epochs in the history of the church. Most of these are discussed in other chapters. The events most influential to our present-day patterns of worship include:

The decline of the use of Latin hymns and ritual (fourteenth century).

The Reformation, which brought about congregational singing (sixteenth century).

The birth of hymns of human composure.

The birth of the gospel song in evangelism.

The standardization of the organ as a church instrument.

Concepts of Public Worship

Two different concepts of worship are found among Protestant churches today: the liturgical and the free.

1. Liturgical worship. This type of worship adheres to a strict order of service known as a ritual. It was developed primarily during the Middle Ages and adopted by Martin Luther and his followers in the Reformation. The ritual consists of prayers by the minister, musical responses by the choir and the congregation, and active participation of the people in reading litanies of prayer, supplication and dedication, in the observance of communion and in listening to the Word of God. Carl Halter explains liturgical worship thus: "The various items included . . . are calculated to make the worshiper aware of his natural sinful condition, to bring him the good news of God's free grace in Christ, and to apply this grace to the individual worshiper in the most personal way possible by means of Holy Communion."[1]

The liturgy is based on the liturgical year, which is a division

---

[1] C. Halter, *The Practice of Sacred Music* (St. Louis: Concordia Publishing House, 1956), p. 27.

of the Sundays of the church year according to the events in the life and ministry of the Lord as follows:

Advent—the four Sundays preceding Christmas Sunday, emphasizing the prophecy and events leading to the birth of Christ

Christmas—the Sunday preceding Christmas Day

Christmastide—the two Sundays after Christmas

Epiphany—the third Sunday after Christmas (near January 6, the day of the Epiphany), commemorating the visit of the Wise Men

Sundays after Epiphany—dealing with the early life of Christ

Septuagesima, Sexagesima, Quinquagesima—the three Sundays before Lent, emphasizing events foretelling Christ's coming death

Lent—from Ash Wednesday to Holy Week, dealing with events leading up to Christ's death

Holy Week—the week preceding Easter

Easter—celebrating Christ's resurrection

Eastertide—Sundays after Easter, treating the last events of Christ's life on earth

Ascension—sixth Sunday after Easter, relating the account of the ascension of Christ

Whitsunday—two Sundays after the ascension, commemorating Pentecost

Trinity—the following Sunday, emphasizing the threefold nature of God

Sundays after Trinity—dealing with general subjects relating to the Christian life

Other Sundays, such as Thanksgiving, All Saints' Day, Transfiguration Sunday, and some national events, are also observed in some denominations.

Scripture texts, known as "pericope texts," are established as the basis for the sermons and Scripture readings to be followed for each Sunday. The biblical selections, known as the lectionary, include an Old Testament account, a Gospel selection, and usually another portion from one of the epistles, compiled for each Sunday of the year by a special committee on worship in each denomination. The following is a listing of pericope texts observed one year by the Evangelical Covenant Church in America.

PERICOPE TEXTS
(OLD TESTAMENT, EPISTLE AND GOSPEL TEXTS)

January 6 — Epiphany
Isa. 60; II Cor. 3:18—4:6;
Matt. 12:14-21

January 13 — 1st Sunday After
Epiphany
Isa. 55; Heb. 2:11-16; Matt.
12:46-50

January 20 — 2nd Sunday After
Epiphany
Isa. 41:1-20; Eph. 6:1-4; Luke
19:1-10

January 27 — 3rd Sunday After
Epiphany
Prov. 2; II Thess. 2:13-17;
Matt. 8:14-17

February 3 — 4th Sunday After
Epiphany
Prov. 3; II Tim. 1:7-10; Matt.
14:22-33

February 10 — Septuagesima
Sunday
Gen. 1:1-19; Phil. 3:7-14; Luke
17:7-10

February 17 — Sexagesima
Sunday
Gen. 2:4-17; II Tim. 3:10—4:5;
Matt. 10:2-16

February 24 — Quinquagesima
Sunday
Gen. 4:1-16; I Cor. 1:20-25;
Mark 10:32-45

February 27 — Ash Wednesday
Isa. 58:1-12; Heb. 12:1-14;
Luke 15

March 3 — 1st Sunday in Lent
Isa. 58; Heb. 4:15, 16; Luke
10:17-20

March 10 — 2nd Sunday in Lent
Gen. 8; Heb. 5:5, 7-9; Mark
9:14-32

March 17 — 3rd Sunday in Lent
Gen. 11:1-9; Col. 1:24-29;
Luke 4:31-37

March 24 — 4th Sunday in Lent
Gen. 13; Phil. 3:7-15; John
6:52-66

March 31 — 5th Sunday in Lent
Exodus 2:1-22; II Cor. 1:3-7;
John 8:31-45

April 7 — Palm Sunday
Zech. 9:9-14; Heb. 8:8-12;
Luke 12:14-22

April 14 — Easter Sunday
Exodus 12:1-14; Eph. 1:15-23;
Matt. 28:1-8

April 21 — 1st Sunday After
Easter
Exodus 14:1-22; Acts 13:32-41;
John 21:15-23

April 28 — 2nd Sunday After
Easter
Lev. 6:1-13; Rev. 21:10-14,
21-27; John 10:1-10

May 5 — 3rd Sunday After
Easter
Lev. 19:1-18; I Peter 1:3-8;
John 14:1-12

May 12 — 4th Sunday After
Easter
Lev. 23:1-14; I John 3:18-24;
John 15:10-17

May 19 — 5th Sunday After
Easter
Lev. 26:1-17; Rev. 3:14-22;
Luke 11:1-13

May 23 — Ascension Day
II Kings 2:1-15; Rom. 8:34-39;
Luke 24:49-53

May 26 — 6th Sunday After
Easter
Dan. 7:9-14; Rom. 8:26-28;
John 15:18-25

June 2 — Whitsunday
(Pentecost)
Isa. 11:1-10; Acts 2:37-47;
John 14:15-21

June 9 — Trinity Sunday
Isa. 6:1-8; Col. 1:9-23; Matt.
28:18-20

June 16 — 1st Sunday After
Trinity

Joshua 1; I Tim. 6:6-19; Matt. 16:24-27

June 23 — 2ND SUNDAY AFTER TRINITY
Joshua 4:1-14; Hosea 11:1-7; Luke 9:51-62

June 30 — 3RD SUNDAY AFTER TRINITY
Joshua 6:1-20; Eph. 2:1-10; Matt. 9:9-13

July 7 — 4TH SUNDAY AFTER TRINITY
Joshua 8:1-20; Rom. 14:1-18; Luke 13:1-5

July 14 — 5TH SUNDAY AFTER TRINITY
Joshua 20; Acts 26:1-29; Matt. 16:13-20

July 21 — 6TH SUNDAY AFTER TRINITY
Joshua 24:1-15; James 2:8-17; Matt. 5:38-42

July 28 — 7TH SUNDAY AFTER TRINITY
Joshua 24:16-28; Rev. 1:9-18; Matt. 17:9-13

August 4 — 8TH SUNDAY AFTER TRINITY (TRANSFIGURATION)
Judges 5; I John 4:1-6; Matt. 7:22-29

August 11 — 9TH SUNDAY AFTER TRINITY
Judges 7:1-21; II Thess. 3:10-13; Luke 16:10-15

August 18 — 10TH SUNDAY AFTER TRINITY
Judges 11:1-11, 29-40; Heb. 3:12-19; Matt. 11:20-24

August 25 — 11TH SUNDAY AFTER TRINITY
Ruth 1:1-17; I John 1:8—2:2; Matt. 23:1-12

September 1 — 12TH SUNDAY AFTER TRINITY
Ruth 2:1-17; I Cor. 2:9-16; Matt. 5:33-37

September 8 — 13TH SUNDAY AFTER TRINITY
I Sam. 3; II Cor. 9:6-10; Mark 12:41-44

September 15 — 14TH SUNDAY AFTER TRINITY
I Sam. 4:1-18; I Tim. 1:12-17; Matt. 11:25-30

September 22 — 15TH SUNDAY AFTER TRINITY
I Sam. 9:1-20; I Cor. 7:29-31; Matt. 6:19-23

September 29 — 16TH SUNDAY AFTER TRINITY
I Sam. 10:1-9, 17-27; Phil. 1:19-26; John 5:19-21

October 6 — 17TH SUNDAY AFTER TRINITY
I Sam. 16:1-13; Gal. 5:1-14; John 8:31-36

October 13 — 18TH SUNDAY AFTER TRINITY
I Sam. 17:1-11, 32-49; I John 2:7-17; Mark 10:17-27

October 20 — 19TH SUNDAY AFTER TRINITY
I Sam. 18:1-16; Rom. 7:14-25; John 7:40-52

October 27 — REFORMATION SUNDAY
I Sam. 24; I Peter 2:3-9; Matt. 21:33-46

November 3 — 21ST SUNDAY AFTER TRINITY (ALL SAINTS)
II Sam. 1:1-12, 17-27; Rom. 5:1-8; John 10:22-30

November 10 — 22ND SUNDAY AFTER TRINITY
II Sam. 7:1-17; I Thess. 5:14-23; Mark 4:21-25

November 17 — 23RD SUNDAY AFTER TRINITY
II Sam. 12:1-10, 15-23; Rom. 13:1-7; Matt. 17:24-27

November 24 — 24TH SUNDAY AFTER TRINITY (JUDGMENT)
Eccles. 11:9—12:14; Rev. 20:11—21:7; Matt. 13:47-50

December 1 — 1ST SUNDAY IN ADVENT
Isa. 40:1-11; Rom. 13:11-14; Matt. 21:1-9

December 8 — 2ND SUNDAY IN
ADVENT
Isa. 55; Rom. 15:4-13; Luke
21:25-36

December 15 — 3RD SUNDAY IN
ADVENT
Isa. 35; I Cor. 4:1-5; Matt.
11:2-10

December 22 — 4TH SUNDAY IN
ADVENT
Isa. 9:2-7; Phil. 4:4-7; John
1:19-28

December 29 — SUNDAY AFTER
CHRISTMAS
Isa. 63:7-17; Gal. 4:1-7; Luke
2:33-40

—*Reprinted with permission*

2. Free-type worship. This procedure of worship was first practiced by the early followers of Christ, who assembled informally outside the temple, without following any apparent order of service. They gathered wherever Christ appeared, and probably spent the entire time listening to His teachings and asking Him questions. Free-type worship is most frequently practiced by denominations or groups of Christians who have reacted against meaningless customs and rituals carried on by churches that do not emphasize the true message of redemption through Jesus Christ. Its pattern was greatly influenced by the early Calvinistic movement and also by the English severance from the Roman church, at which time all candles, incense, statues and altars were destroyed, and worship forms, litanies and music were discarded, since they were haunting reminders of the corruption experienced in the church under Roman domination.

Problems Faced in Planning a Worship Service

There are dangers to be recognized when planning or conducting a worship service, whether it be liturgical or free. Some of the most prevalent ones are as follows:

Liturgical Worship
1. Too much organization may tend to prohibit the free working of the Holy Spirit.
2. Too much participation may detract from the worshiper's inner reflection and thought.
3. Too much week-by-week repetition may render the acts of worship meaningless.
4. Too much reliance upon prescribed texts may prohibit special emphases often desired in the local church.

Free-Type Worship
1. Too little organization may cause the loss of a continuity of worship.
2. Too little active participation may make the worshiper nothing more than a spectator.
3. Too much informality could become distracting and confusing.
4. Too little organization of messages may lead to overemphasis of favorite themes and sermon texts and a neglect of other important ones.

Needs of the Worshiper

It would be a mistake to suggest that either practice of worship is better than the other. The most important things to consider are the ingredients which are necessary to lead a person into an act of worship. These can be realized in either the liturgical or the free-type worship service if properly prepared and conducted. It must be remembered, however, that a good balance is necessary and that all the following needs should be provided for within the order of service:

1. Time to meditate quietly before God, undistracted by external things. This is especially essential in the beginning stages of worship.

2. Opportunity to take part actively in corporate worship. This can be through responsive readings, recitation of an affirmation of faith, the Apostles' Creed or the Lord's Prayer.

3. Opportunity to express exuberant praises to God, through hymns of praise, the Gloria Patri or the Doxology.

4. Time to bow in penitence and supplication, during pastoral prayers and choral responses.

5. Opportunity to receive instruction in the Word of God, through the sermon, Scripture lesson, doctrinal hymn and anthem.

6. Opportunity to dedicate oneself to God.

7. Challenge to leave the place of worship with new determinations and added assurance of God's presence and power.

The Service of Worship

The well-balanced worship service can be conducted in many different ways and may assume various orders. Even a church which practices free-type worship usually has an order which is followed quite consistently from week to week. The accompanying examples of free and liturgical services will more clearly indicate the diversified ways in which worship can be conducted.

1. An example of a nonliturgical worship service

MORNING WORSHIP
(First Sunday in Lent)
ADORATION

Organ Prelude

Call to Worship
> Breathe on me, Breath of God,
>> Fill me with life anew,
> That I may love what Thou dost love,
>> And do what Thou wouldst do.

Invocation
Hymn of Adoration
Affirmation of Faith   Apostles' Creed
Anthem

MEDITATION

Responsive Reading
Gloria Patri
Pastoral Prayer
Lord's Prayer
Choral Response
Hymn of Meditation
Scripture Lesson
Sermon

DEDICATION

Worship with Tithes and Offerings
Hymn of Dedication
Benediction
Congregation United in Silent Prayer
Organ Postlude

2. An example of a liturgical order of service

THIRD SUNDAY IN LENT

Tower Chimes
Prelude
Opening Hymn and Processional
Invocation
Confession of Sins
Introit for the Day
Gloria Patri
Kyrie
Gloria in Excelsis
Collect for the Day
Epistle for the Day
Lenten Sentence
Gospel for the Day
Apostles' Creed
Announcements
Anthem
Sermon
Offering
Offertory Solo

Offertory Hymn
Prayer of the Church
Lord's Prayer
Closing Hymn
Benediction
Recessional Hymn
Postlude

3. Portion of the liturgical service of the Lutheran Church in America

THE SERVICE

¶ *The General Rubrics contain directions additional to those which appear in the service.*

¶ *Intonations provided for the Minister's parts of the Service represent a permissive use. They are not to be considered directive.*

¶ *The preparatory office up to the Introit may be said. If it be sung, the following musical setting may be used.*

¶ *The Congregation shall rise. The Minister shall sing or say:*

IN the Name of the Father, and of the Son, and of the Holy Ghost.

¶. *The Congregation shall sing or say:*
A - men.

A - men.

THE CONFESSION OF SINS

¶ *The Minister shall say:*

BELOVED in the Lord! Let us draw near with a true heart, and confess our sins unto God our Father, beseeching him, in the Name of our Lord Jesus Christ, to grant us forgiveness.

¶ *The Minister and Congregation may kneel.*
¶ *They shall sing or say:*

Minister	Congregation
Our help is in the Name of the Lord.	R. Who made heaven and earth.
Minister	Congregation
I said, I will confess my transgressions unto the Lord.	R. And thou forgavest the iniquity of my sin.

Minister — Our help is in the Name of the Lord. R⁺. Who made heaven and earth

Minister — I said, I will confess my transgressions unto the Lord. R⁺. And thou forgavest the iniquity of my sin.

¶ *Then shall the Minister say:*

ALMIGHTY God, our Maker and Redeemer, we poor sinners confess unto thee, that we are by nature sinful and unclean, and that we have sinned against thee by thought, word, and deed. Wherefore we flee for refuge to thine infinite mercy, seeking and imploring thy grace, for the sake of our Lord Jesus Christ.

¶ *The Congregation shall say with the Minister:*

O MOST merciful God, who hast given thine only-begotten Son to die for us, have mercy upon us, and for his sake grant us remission of all our sins: and by thy Holy Spirit increase in us true knowledge of thee and of thy will, and true obedience to thy Word, that by thy grace we may come to everlasting life; through Jesus Christ our Lord. Amen.

¶ *Then the Minister, standing, and facing the Congregation, shall say:*

ALMIGHTY God, our heavenly Father, hath had mercy upon us, and hath given his only Son to die for us, and for his sake forgiveth us all our sins. To them that believe on his Name, he giveth power to become the sons of God, and bestoweth upon them his Holy Spirit. He that believeth, and is baptized, shall be saved. Grant this, O Lord, unto us all.

¶ *Or, he may say:*

THE Almighty and merciful God grant unto you, being penitent, pardon and remission of all your sins, time for amendment of life, and the grace and comfort of his Holy Spirit.

¶ *The Congregation shall sing or say:*
A - men.

A - men.

—*From the Service Book and Hymnal of the Lutheran Church in America, by permission of the Commission on the Liturgy and Hymnal.*

Note that the preceding orders of worship are divided into worship sections. Each of these contributes to one or more of the previously mentioned needs of the worshiper, and they all incorporate the two primary aspects of adoration and submission. The distinguishing factors in these orders of worship are the sequences used and the amount of extra features employed. These are usually determined by:

a. Length of the service.

b. Background of the congregation, culturally and socially.

c. Denominational affiliations and their commonly accepted practices.

d. Personal preferences of the minister.

e. Facilities and personnel available (organ, choir, soloists).

The Musical Portions of a Worship Service

Each musical part of the worship service has its own distinct ministry. The following is an outline of the music more frequently found in worship services, with a general evaluation of the contribution to be made by each:

Prelude. This is the "curtain" between the outside world and the inner chamber of private worship. It should be such that will permit personal meditation for the believer, while aiding in the creating of an atmosphere conducive to worship. It could be a familiar hymn tune or medley, but familiarity is not necessary. Many of the standard organ and piano classics make good prelude material and often contribute greatly due to their neutral qualities.

Processional. This is either sung by the choir or the congregation, or played by the organ or piano. It changes to a more stately mood than the prelude, and denotes the beginning of corporate worship. A good well-timed entry of choir and ministers adds greatly to the dignity of this part of the service.

Call to worship. Usually the Gloria Patri, the Doxology, or a hymn such as "Holy, Holy, Holy" is used. This begins the "ascription of God's worth," reminding the worshiper of the greatness of God.

Opening hymn. After the worshipers have been reminded of God's greatness, they then sing a hymn of praise to God.

Choral response to prayer. The choir now represents the congregation in pronouncing their affirmation upon the prayer offered by the minister. This part of the service can be especially meaningful if its purpose is clearly understood.

Anthem. This is an opportunity to present scriptural and doctrinal truths enhanced by musical settings. The type of anthem will vary week after week, presenting thoughts of praise, meditation, challenge, comfort, or subjective themes relating to the season or the message of the hour.

Doxology or offertory sentence (before or after offering). This is to remind the worshiper of the goodness of God when giving the tithes and offerings. Giving is a definite part of the second aspect of worship, that of submission.

Offertory. This is either played on the organ or piano, or sung by the choir or a soloist. It should not be considered a mere fill-in while the offering is being taken, but should give textual material that will provoke thought or meditation, or be mediative in character.

Solo (or choir, quartet, etc.) before sermon. Being the final musical medium of preparing hearts for the message, this should be subjective and thought-provoking.

Hymn after sermon. This is a time of heart-searching, when definite personal responses are being made. This hymn should be in keeping with the sermon subject and possibly be chosen by the minister himself.

Choral benediction. Once again, the choir represents the people. After the minister has bidden Godspeed to each member by means of the benediction, the choir then pronounces God's blessing on the congregation. All are about to return to worldly cares and problems after having met with God.

Postlude. Like the prelude, this serves as a curtain between the inner chamber and the outside world. It should be challenging and assuring, should give the members of the congregation confidence as they reenter the activities of their daily lives.

Music Used in Worship

A worship service is no more dependent upon great music than on elaborate church architecture or well-developed sermons. It may take place within the simplest surroundings and through the simplest forms and means. The important factor in choosing hymns, anthems, solos and other musical selections for the service is not their level of difficulty but their appropriateness for the occasion.

1. Worshipful and meaningful texts. Except for the selections which immediately precede and follow the sermon, the music does not need to follow the theme of the message of the hour. It is more significant if it contributes to worship.

It is important, however, to avoid any musical texts which appear to be in opposition to the message contents, such as a song entitled "Turn Back, O Man" following a sermon on "Pressing Toward the Mark."

In order that the congregation can experience, through singing, the two aspects of worship, every service should contain some hymns of outright expression of praise and others of dedication. The anthem and other musical selections can also be based on one of these aspects, or can be more subjective and in keeping with the message or season of the church year if this seems more desirable.

Services with special topics, such as foreign missions, Christmas, Thanksgiving, Pentecost and others, will obviously call for a greater emphasis on subjective music.

2. Communicative yet elevating music. Music will not contribute to worship unless it communicates. Care must be taken to prevent the overuse of styles and idioms not understood by the average church member. This does not imply a necessity for lowering musical standards; neither does it suggest that only one type of music should be used. The wise choice of music should both communicate and elevate.

It should consist of a proper balance of:
 familiar and unfamiliar hymn tunes
 accepted forms and new idioms
 bright and quiet pieces
 simple and more complex styles
 direct and more abstract treatments of texts.

It is not to be expected that such a balanced diet of music will communicate to everyone all the time. On the other hand, it should challenge each member of the congregation to learn to understand and appreciate new musical forms of worship and, as a result, discover new heights in his own worship experience. If handled judiciously, this can be accomplished without deterring from his present act of worship.

Summary and Conclusion

The primary function of music in the church service is to lead each member of the congregation to worship. This requires communication. The secondary goal is to seek to both expand and elevate his concepts of worship by challenging him with music which provides opportunity for deeper spiritual thought. This stimulates spiritual growth and Christian maturity. Therefore, the goal is not to "raise musical standards." It is rather to give the worshiper that which will draw him closer to God, command the best from his Christian life and give him a deeper and greater concept of God. Although other dangers have been previously cited, there is none so great as that mentioned by Christ himself: "Ye worship ye know not what." The music used in worship must help the worshiper discover and understand what he worships, or, better still, *whom* he worships.

RECOMMENDED READING

Ashton, J. N. *Music in Worship*. Boston: Pilgrim Press, 1943.

Bacon, Allan. *The True Function of Church Music*. Stockton, Calif.: Printwell Press, 1953.

Blackwood, A. W. *The Fine Art of Public Worship*. Nashville: Abingdon Press, 1934.

Halter, Carl, *The Practice of Sacred Music*. St. Louis: Concordia Publishing House, 1955.

Pratt, W. S. *Musical Ministries in the Church*. New York: G. Schirmer, Inc., 1923.

Sydnor, James R. *Planning for Church Music*. Nashville: Abingdon Press, 1961.

Urang, Gunnar. *Church Music—For the Glory of God*. Moline, Ill.: Christian Service Foundation. 1956.

Chapter 3

MUSIC IN CHRISTIAN EDUCATION

Introduction

The department of Christian education consists of all the educational activities in the church program, including the Sunday school, youth fellowships, children's churches, vacation Bible school, boys' and girls' clubs, scout troops, athletic programs, leadership training and adult education classes. The graded choirs and instrumental groups are also closely affiliated and in some churches are actually a part of the department. Whether or not they are directly related in the organizational plan, both the music and the Christian education activities have the same ideals and goals. To be sure, music is a form of Christian education, distinguished from the other functions only because of its particular medium of education, music.

Background of Christian Education

According to Jewish historians Philo and Josephus, group-training in the teachings of the Word of God took place as far back as the time of Moses. Beginning at an early age, youth would gather to hear and learn the laws of God as taught by their fathers in response to the command given them by Moses in Deuteronomy 6:6, 7: "These words, which I command thee this day, shall be in thine heart: and thou shalt teach them diligently unto thy children." During the time of David and Solomon, the educational activities were transferred to the temple, which had by then become the center of worship. This training included "the reciting of scriptures, praying, various types of singing, and discussion and explanaton of the Scriptures that had great value in helping the people to understand the way of the Lord more perfectly."[1] Later, probably during the Babylonian captivity, the synagogue arose to become the center of both religious and secular education.

---

[1]Price, Chapman, Tibbs, Carpenter, *A Survey of Religious Education* (New York: Thomas Nelson and Sons, 1940), p. 31.

The New Testament gives evidences that doctors of the law were still teaching in the temple when Christ lived on the earth. Luke 2:46 records the time when, at the age of twelve, Christ had audience with some of these men, and was "both hearing them, and asking them questions." Matthew 4:23 speaks of Christ teaching in the synagogues of Galilee, thereby suggesting that the synagogues were still being used as centers of religious training.

Christian education actually began under the leadership of Jesus Christ himself. His ministry was primarily that of teaching, and He is referred to as a teacher forty-five times in the four Gospels. "He not only taught the masses but also trained a group of teachers who were to carry on when He was gone."[2] In obedience to Jesus' Great Commission, the disciples went forth to "teach all nations" (Matt. 28:19), thus continuing the work which he had begun.

The catechumenal and catechetical schools "represent the first efforts in early Christianity to utilize educational means for Christian promotion."[3] Both were designed to teach Christian principles to new converts as well as to children. However, the catechumenal schools were conducted less formally than the catechetical schools, which were an outgrowth of the dissatisfaction with the pagan philosophical teachings at the universities of the second century and therefore more academic in approach. These schools were replaced in the sixth century by monastic schools, which, in addition to training monks, opened their doors to children seeking a liberal education. At the same time, cathedral schools were established to offer religious training on both the elementary and secondary levels, thus setting a pattern on which the schools of the Reformation were built. The influence and effectiveness of cathedral school education in both moral and religious activity still stand today. It was, however, during the Reformation that the teaching aspect of the church's ministry reached its highest level of importance, since Luther himself depended upon religious training to propagate the truths so long neglected by the Roman church.

It was not until the time of the Protestant Reformation under Luther that the teaching of the Bible once again became a part of the church's ministry. Since then, Christian education has increasingly grown in importance in the Christian church.

One of the greatest Christian education movements was the

[2] *Op. cit.,* p. 37.
[3] *Op. cit.,* p. 50.

organization of Sunday schools. This movement began in Gloucester, England, in the middle of the 18th century, and became established in America in 1785, only two years after Britain declared the thirteen colonies to be free. Under the personal endorsement of many influential leaders, such as Wesley in England and Moody in America, the movement soon grew in numbers and effectiveness.

The twentieth century has witnessed several newer developments in the areas of youth organizations, Bible clubs and Bible camps, as well as an increased emphasis on adult education programs.

The Functions of Music in Christian Education

Although there are many facets to the program of Christian education, its two primary functions are to win (evangelistic function) and to train (educational function). The underlying purpose of using music in Christian education is to fulfill these functions. The Word of God is taught through hymns and choruses which are based on Scripture. Theology, church doctrines, discipleship, Christian ethics and Christian service are all implanted into hearts and minds through the use of church music. These spiritual truths are made clear through their association with melodies, harmonies and rhythms which are expressive and communicative to young and old alike. Active participation is encouraged through group singing, and attitudes of worship and reverence are developed through the quality of music used.

Specific functions through which music ministers within the Christian education program are:

1. *The teaching of hymnody.* The teaching of hymns plays an important part in the preparation of the child to take his place in the adult worship service. It should therefore be approached in a systematic way. Clarence H. Benson, who refers to the establishing of the International Uniform Lessons in 1872 as the "greatest single step ever taken by the Sunday school," further suggests that "a graded course in sacred song may be covered just as effectively as a graded curriculum of the Bible."[4]

In developing such a curriculum, the hymns should be:

a. Selected primarily from the church hymnal, and should include all the "service music" (Doxology, Gloria Patri, etc.) in the worship service.

b. Graded according to difficulty and used year after year in the

---

[4] Clarence H. Benson, *The Sunday School in Action* (Chicago: Moody Press, 1948), p. 81.

same Sunday school department, rotating the relearning of the hymns on a three-year plan.

c. Introduced in the Sunday school and incorporated into the primary and junior church services, youth fellowships and clubs. This kind of repetition is not only vital to learning but also welcomed by boys and girls.

d. Committed to memory by way of a hymn-of-the-month plan, which should be coordinated with the three-year hymn rotation system.

It is not expecting too much to require each child to memorize at least ten new hymns each year, beginning at the primary age and continuing through high school. Although it may be advisable to require the primary children to memorize only one or two stanzas of each, older children should be able to learn entire hymns. The lists of graded hymns at the end of this chapter should serve as a guide in developing such a program. If the hymnal of the church is inadequate, or if the purchase of new hymnals is anticipated, other hymns should be added from time to time.

2. *The use of expressive and subjective songs.* Well-chosen songs or choruses will contribute to the teaching of practical truths relating to the Sunday school lessons and Christian experiences.

a. For the preschool child: songs with actions help picture simple truths about God's love and objects of nature.

b. For primaries and juniors: occasional songs or choruses based on attitudes of worship, prayer, Bible stories or complete Scripture passages will help them develop concepts of worship, Bible study and prayer.

c. For the junior high and high school youth: judiciously selected songs or choruses based on personal experiences in the Christian life will help them meet the challenges facing them in today's complex society. The cardinal principle for choosing such songs should be: always reverent, often picturesque, never trite.

Except for the preschool department, such songs should not constitute more than one-fourth of the singing done each week in the Sunday school and youth fellowships, as the use of the great hymns of the church will be of lasting value and a more meaningful experience.

3. *The encouragement of participation.* The talents of the child need proving, and there is no more natural place to test them than in the Christian education activities, where Bible knowledge and spiritual experience are also being put to the test, nurtured and developed. Children and youth should be given opportunity to use

whatever talents they may have in the primary and junior church or in the youth and club activities. Perhaps some of the talents may also be utilized in the Sunday school worship period, but time limit is usually a factor during that hour.

4. *The development of attitudes.* Attitudes of reverence and respect are affected by:

a. The choice of music used. What we sing, and how we sing it, reveals what we believe and how we treasure it. A poorly chosen song with a weak text or confusing terminologies can easily result in an attitude of indifference to the message or a misconception of the truth. Both are dangerous outcomes. By the same token, the use of mediocre or trivial music can result in an attitude of irreverence or a natural association of the worship of God with mediocrity. A child's musical taste has often been described as a blank page whereon anything may be inscribed. It is the responsibility of the leaders in Christian education to implant good taste for music which is used to worship God. It is not wise to base the selection of songs on the emotional appeal they might have on the children. This may inadvertently lead to the development of poor attitudes toward God as well as the church and its program.

b. The manner in which music is sung. Even at a very young age a child should be taught the importance of singing with reverence. It is inconsistent to ask him to sing as loudly as he can during a hymn of meditation or prayer. It is equally wrong to let him sing a hymn of joy without expressing this feeling through bright, happy tones.

Children should be made conscious of key words in the hymns. The names Jesus, God, Christ and other expressions of Deity should always be sung with love and respect, seeking to avoid such cheap phrases as "Oh, Lordy" and syncopated utterances such as "Do, Lord." In addition to words of Deity, expressive words, such as joy, love, peace, life and death should also be interpreted in their proper manner. This discipline should help the children develop sensitivity toward the texts of hymns from the very first time they sing them.

Uniting the Efforts of Music and Christian Education

There are many ways in which the music program of the church enters into the Christian education functions. At times these areas of overlap may become points of contention, or cause the youth to think he must make a choice between the two. The proper coordination of these functions and the interworking of the two departments will quickly solve any such problems which may occur, and will be of mutual benefit to both departments. Here are some of the ways in which this may be done.

1. *Through correlating the curricula and materials used.* This may include:

a. The use of the same hymn memorization program in the choirs and in the Sunday school.

b. The presentation of combined awards for achievements in both types of activities.

c. The use of the graded choirs in Sunday school festivals and programs.

d. The use of the children's choirs in children's church and youth services.

e. The combining of social functions and the incorporating of choir rehearsals and youth activities.

f. The use of the same sponsors for both music and Christian education functions.

2. *By combining the departments.* Many churches today are following the pattern of the early choir schools, combining all the youth efforts into one concentrated program such as is suggested in the following plan:

Saturday Morning	Primary	Junior	Junior High
9:30—10:15	Bible club	Handcraft	Choir
10:20—11:05	Recreation or handcraft	Choir	Bible club*
11:10—11:55	Choir	Bible club	Handcraft* projects and discussion

* These two periods may be devoted to confirmation classes if desired.

This type of program can be advantageous in many ways, in that it cuts down on personnel needed for leadership, restricts its activities to one day (or evening) in the week, and makes it convenient for parents who must transport their children to the church. Although the plan is designed for three age groups and for Saturday morning, other similar plans could be made to suit the church's need.

3. *Through interdepartmental training programs.* As early as 1914, Sunday schools were experimenting with adult education

programs wherein special courses were offered in many areas of Christian living, Bible study, family care, church history, hymnology and so on. A cooperative effort between the two departments would be mutually beneficial, in that those actively engaged in Christian education could receive training in song leadership, hymn playing, accompanying and other practical areas, while those participating in the music program would be given opportunity to enrich their lives through the study of courses on the Bible, church activities and other related subjects.

There are many ways in which training classes can be worked into the busy church schedule. The following ways are only a few which have been tried and proved practical.

a. A series of six sessions, one evening a week or on Saturday.

b. A rotating curriculum conducted in the adult department of the Sunday school, with two or more courses offered simultaneously for a three-month term.

c. A special music week, in which courses or lectures are given each evening in conjunction with varied musical concerts or other programs.

Source of Material and Personnel

If the church lacks in competent instructors to teach the courses desired, a nearby college or larger church may be able to supply or recommend leaders who qualify. It may also be able to suggest textbooks and materials which could be used. It is possible to purchase course outlines prepared by extension schools, publishers of church supplies, or denominational headquarters. Often these courses may also be taken on a group plan through a correspondence school, wherein the classes would be conducted by a local pastor, music director or layman, but the lessons would be graded by the correspondence school and returned in time for the next lesson. This plan also enables those who are interested to receive school credits.

No church desiring to nurture its membership in musical, biblical and practical training need feel that it is impossible to realize this goal. With material so readily available through the sources mentioned, every church should consider the manifold benefits which would be derived, both for the church and for the individual layman, through such a program.

Music to Be Used in Christian Education

It has been pointed out that if a proper program of hymn learning and memorization were conducted in the Sunday school, the children would soon become well equipped to participate in the adult worship services of the church. The following is a suggested nucleus of hymns and gospel songs which could be learned and used throughout all the Christian education activities. The lists may be augmented by other worthy songs and choruses which will aid in the teaching of certain lessons and basic Christian truths. These lists should not be considered exhaustive but should rather be used as a guide to the choosing of other hymns found in the church hymnal. A child can never learn too many hymns. With each one he learns he embraces a new vocabulary and a fresh approach to self-expression. As he memorizes new hymn texts, he strengthens his concept of Christian principles. As Andrew Law once said, "Theology and music move on hand in hand into time, and will continue eternally to illustrate, embellish, enforce, impress and fix in the mind the grand and great truths of Christianity." Hymnody is man's way of personally defining and expressing his theological beliefs and his Christian experiences.

Beginner Department—Ages 4-5

Away in a Manger—(attributed to Luther)
Can a Little Child Like Me?—Basswood
Gentle Jesus, Meek and Mild—Shaw
In Our Work and in Our Play—Unknown
Jesus Bids Us Shine—Excell
Jesus Loves Even Me—Bliss
Jesus Loves Me—Bradbury
Jesus Wants Me for a Sunbeam—Excell
Silent Night, Holy Night—Gruber

Primary Department—Ages 6-8

Christ Arose—Lowry
Doxology—Bourgeois
Holy Bible, Book Divine—Bradbury
I Need Thee Every Hour—Lowry
Joy to the World—Handel
Now Thank We All Our God—Cruger
Saviour, Like a Shepherd Lead Us—Bradbury
Stand Up for Jesus—Webb
Tell Me the Stories of Jesus—Challinor
Tell Me the Story of Jesus—Sweney
Thy Word Is Like a Garden, Lord—Fink
What a Friend We Have in Jesus—Converse

JUNIOR DEPARTMENT—Ages 9-11

Fairest Lord Jesus—Willis
Gloria Patri—Meineke
Holy, Holy, Holy—Dykes
I Would Be True—Peek
My Faith Looks Up to Thee—Mason
Nearer, My God, to Thee—Mason
Rock of Ages—Hastings
Take My Life, and Let It Be—Malan
This Is My Father's World—Sheppard
Thy Word Have I Hid in My Heart—Sellers
We Gather Together—Netherlands melody
When Morning Gilds the Skies—Barnby

INTERMEDIATE (JUNIOR HIGH) DEPARTMENT
Ages 12-14

All Creatures of Our God and King—arranged
All Hail the Power of Jesus' Name—(Coronation tune)
Come, Thou Almighty King—Giardini
Crown Him with Many Crowns—Elvey
For the Beauty of the Earth—arr. from Kocher
How Firm a Foundation—Anon.
Jesus Calls Us—Jude
Love Divine, All Loves Excelling—Zundel
O Master, Let Me Walk with Thee—Schumann
O Zion, Haste—Walch
The Church's One Foundation—Wesley
When I Survey the Wondrous Cross—arr. Mason

HIGH SCHOOL DEPARTMENT—Ages 15-18

A Charge to Keep I Have—Mason
A Mighty Fortress—Luther
All Glory, Laud and Honor—Teschner
Dear Lord and Father of Mankind—Maker
For All the Saints—Williams
Glorious Things of Thee Are Spoken—Haydn
Jesus, Lover of My Soul—Marsh
O Sacred Head—Bach
Rejoice, Ye Pure in Heart—Messiter
The Spacious Firmament—Haydn
The Strife Is O'er—Palestrina
When, His Salvation Bringing—Tours

Music to Avoid in Christian Education

Although music has long been accepted as an important tool of Christian education, the songs which are sometimes used place great limitations upon its effectiveness. In the past three centuries there has been an evident lack of quality and consistency in children's music. One of the earlier examples of this in the English language was *Divine and Moral Songs,* published by Isaac Watts in 1720. Although this songbook did contain many excellent texts, it also included some highly questionable ones, as exemplified by the following excerpt:

> Let dogs delight to bark and bite,
>   For God hath made them so;
> Let bears and lions growl and fight,
>   For 'tis their nature, too.
> But, children, you should never let
>   Such angry passions rise;
> Your little hands were never made
>   To tear each other's eyes.[5]

Since that time there have been several inappropriate trends which have found their way into children's music and which should be avoided by Christian educators. They include:

1. Texts which belittle the intellect of the child. "Two things a child despises are to be thought of as little and to be talked down to as inferior."[6] The child needs to sing songs which challenge him to deeper thinking. Texts which oversimplify truths or overuse symbolism will contribute very little to his spiritual growth and understanding, while at the same time having a degrading effect upon his morale. Such texts are not to be confused with those which are simple and understandable to the child without being trite or offensive. Songs which speak the language most understood by the smallest child will of necessity be simple; nevertheless, they can challenge and edify. One example of a simple but challenging text is the following, written in the nineteenth century:

> Jesus bids us shine, with a clear, pure light,
> Like a little candle burning in the night;
> In this world of darkness we must shine,
> You in your small corner, and I in mine.
>   SUSAN WARNER

---

[5] A. C. Lovelace and W. C. Rice, *Music and Worship in the Church* (Nashville: Abingdon Press, 1960), p. 170.

[6] *Loc. cit.*

2. Music which resembles the popular songs of the day. It is difficult to teach a child to discern between that which is spiritual and that which is sinful or degrading. One way to do this is to help him develop an understanding and realization of the extreme differences between the things of God and the less edifying attractions of the world around him. If the music which is used in the Sunday school and youth department sounds like the hit tunes performed by stars of the entertainment industry, a child may develop a lack of respect for the church, an insensitivity to the majesty and dignity of God, and even a feeling that the church sanctions the popular trends commonly associated with the theater, night club, radio and television.

3. Songs which do not relate to the experiences of the child. There are many acceptable gospel songs and hymns which speak of experiences not known or understood by children. Two examples are:

> I was sinking deep in sin,
>   Far from the peaceful shore,
> Very deeply stained within,
>   Sinking to rise no more;
> But the Master of the sea
>   Heard my despairing cry,
> From the waters lifted me,
>   Now safe am I.
>
> JAMES ROWE

> Years I spent in vanity and pride,
> Caring not my Lord was crucified,
> Knowing not it was for me He died
>   On Calvary.
>
> WILLIAM R. NEWELL

Although these verses express the personal testimony of many adults, they do not relate the backgrounds and experiences of the young child. It is unwise to use such songs in the children's departments of the Sunday school. Neither is it realistic to permit the very young child to sing songs which indicate a longing to go to heaven, since life after death is still a mystery to him. The subjects of heaven, the second coming of Christ and life after death should be clearly taught and explained, but the major emphasis should be placed upon the necessity of living for Jesus.

Summary and Conclusion

Christian education seeks to develop the complete person: his spiritual being, his moral and ethical standards, his social life and his cultural tastes. It is therefore concerned with what takes place in his heart and soul, what he does with his life and time, whom he fellowships with from day to day, and what he enjoys listening to, reading and observing. In order to fulfill this great responsibility, the Christian educator should be aware of the fact that, while he is seeking to mold and develop Christian attitudes and principles in his children, a world of fascination and intrigue is attempting to lure them away from God and the church. It is important, therefore, that each child be taught to honor and respect God at a very early age. "Train up a child in the way he should go: and when he is old, he will not depart from it" (Prov. 22:6).

The music which a child is taught in the Sunday school and youth department plays an important part in this program of development. If he has been trained to always sing with reverence when worshiping God, rather than glibly approaching Him as though He were "the friendly man next door," the child will grow and develop in Christian character and stability. He will not only be a more positive prospect for future leadership in the church but will also be less inclined to give in to the lures of the sinful world.

RECOMMENDED READING

LOVELACE, A. C., and RICE, W. C. *Music and Worship in the Church*. Nashville: Abingdon Press, 1960.

MORSCH, VIVIAN. *The Use of Music in Christian Education*. Philadelphia: The Westminster Press, 1956.

THOMAS, EDITH L. *Music in Christian Education*. Nashville: Abingdon Press, 1953.

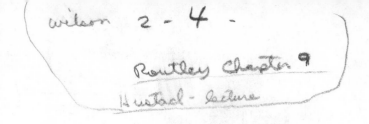
Chapter 4

MUSIC IN EVANGELISM

Introduction

Evangelism is the bearing of the Good News. This Good News
tells of salvation provided through the death and resurrection of
Jesus Christ (John 10:10*b*).

The term "evangelism" is usually associated with special services or campaigns known as evangelistic campaigns or revival services, designed to reach the lost with this great message of salvation.
However, the ministry of evangelism is by no means restricted to
these special efforts alone but is incorporated into all the functions
of the Christian church, from the worship service, through the
Christian education activities and into the ministries of visitation
and personal witness. All these activities are designed to evangelize.

An evangelist is one who carries the Good News to those who
need its message. The first evangelists were the disciples of Jesus,
who were commissioned by Him to "go . . . into all the world,
and preach the gospel to every creature" (Mark 16:15). The
Apostle Paul is often referred to as the greatest evangelist that
has ever lived, and the book of Acts records the three missionary
journeys taken by Paul and other evangelists in response to
Christ's Great Commission. These journeys were ministries of both
evangelism and teaching, two of the spiritual gifts of which Paul
spoke in Ephesians 4:11, as well as two of the three basic ministries of the church today. In Paul's final words to Timothy, he
charged his young associate to "do the work of an evangelist"
(II Tim. 4:5), no doubt commissioning him to carry on the work
in which they had engaged together.

In this study of music in evangelism, primary consideration is
given to its use in the many special efforts of evangelism, both in
the local church and in its wider outreach.

REACHING PEOPLE THROUGH IMPLEMENTS OF EVANGELISM

Functions of the Implements	Desired Goals	Possible Unfavorable Side Effects
1. To communicate to a person's emotions (sense perception)	To attract attention through a personality or an implement, in order to stimulate interest in the message	Too much attention drawn to the person or implement; overstimulation of senses
2. To convey a message (intellectual response)	To reach intellect with the message of salvation, in clarity and with pure motives (I Cor. 2:1, 2)	Lack of integrity or lack of clarity of message; impure motives on the part of the messenger
3. To convince of a need (emotional response)	To attempt to cause a response of soul, indicating an interest in the message, with the possibility of a conversion experience to follow (John 5:24)	Intellectual response to a teaching; physical response to a person; emotional response which appears to be a spiritual response
4. To lead to conversion (response of the will, physical response)	To cause a response of the will to accept the message, forsake the past and receive Christ (Matt. 16:24)	Following a religious teaching or joining a church; following after a person; following the dictates of the will

Implements of Evangelism

The implements most successfully used in evangelistic efforts include music, personal testimony, storytelling (especially in children's meetings), preaching and teaching. These all function through the media of public meetings, radio and television, religious motion pictures and dramas, Sunday school and youth work, personal witness, tract distribution, rescue mission work, and foreign missionary enterprises. All these media have proved to be effective means of evangelizing. In the hands of dedicated workers, under the guidance of God and through the empowering of the Holy Spirit, they help the workers to communicate, convey the message of redemption, convince men of their need and lead them to conversion.

On the other hand, there are dangers of misuse of these media as well. Since they are effective in their powers of communication, they also possess great influence over the sensory responses of man, as discussed in the first chapter. Consequently, the users of the implements must be able to direct these powers in the right manner, and must be sure that they are obtaining the desired goals rather than other unfavorable results. A few examples of possible unfavorable results are cited here.

Whereas the desired goal of a rescue mission ministry is to lead the down-and-outer to Christ, the One who can supply his spiritual needs, some men and women of the street may apparently respond to the message but be doing so only for the sake of receiving a meal, some clean clothing and a place to sleep for the night.

Whereas a church may be desirous of winning men and women of the community to Christ and providing them with a place to worship and to serve God, some may respond to the invitation in order to become a member of the church and thereby gain a certain amount of social distinction and ease of conscience.

Whereas a youth organization may design its program to attract youth and reach them with the message of a new life and future in Christ, some may respond to the message in order to participate in the athletic or social functions conducted by the organization.

The accompanying chart indicates some of the desired goals of the implements of evangelism in light of the four steps of communication previously mentioned. It also suggests some unfavorable results which might occur if the implements are not used properly, or are lacking the power of the Holy Spirit.

Music as an Implement

"As well attempt to run without feet or box without hands as try to conduct evangelistic meetings without music" (Sellers).[1]

Perhaps this is an intentional overstatement, but it rightfully implies the inherent relationship between the psychological powers of music and the other means which are effectively used in evangelism, a relationship which makes them appear almost inseparable. Looking at music in light of the four steps of communication, the following is observed:

1. *Music communicates.* The principal means of communicating to the sensory emotions of man are:

a. The rhythm, harmony and melody of the music.

b. The enthusiasm of the performer.

c. The attractiveness of personality and appearance of the performer.

d. The beauty of tone, style and musicianship displayed in the performance.

It may appear that the personality and the media are overemphasized, but it must be remembered that this is not only a tried and proved method but also a biblically ordained way of obtaining the initial contact of communication with man: "How shall they hear without a preacher?" (Rom. 10:14). The heart of man will seldom respond to a message until his mind is attracted to the messenger and his emotions register a certain degree of satisfactory response to the personality.

2. *Music conveys.* The nature of man's final response to the method of communication is dependent largely upon three things:

a. A positive message. "Ye shall know the truth, and the truth shall make you free" (John 8:32). The message must be clearly and correctly stated, whether it be through words and music which testify of the singer's personal relationship and fellowship with Christ, or through a hymn containing the doctrine of salvation.

b. A pure motive. "He that soweth to his flesh shall of the flesh reap corruption; but he that soweth to the Spirit shall of the Spirit reap life everlasting" (Gal. 6:8). "The human love of elaboration and ornamentation is the curse of sacred song" (Anon.).

c. A clear presentation. "In simplicity and godly sincerity" (II Cor. 1:12). Without clarity and simplicity in the presentation of the text and music, there will be no communication of

---

[1] E. O. Sellers, *How to Improve Church Music* (New York: Fleming H. Revell Co., 1928), p. 140.

message. Clarity demands the vehicles of sincerity, simplicity of style, good diction and correct phrasing. Without clarity, the end result will be nothing more than an emotional response, if any active response occurs at all.

.3. *Music helps to convince.* A proper application of the above implements to the message should result in the following:

a. The rhythm, harmony and melody will convey the text in an understandable way.

b. The beauty of tone and style of performance will add impact to the content of the message.

c. The enthusiasm of the performer will convince the listener of the authenticity of the experience which he claims to have and of which he is singing. In other words, he will sing it as if he means it.

d. The attractiveness of the performer's personality, his appearance and his apparent joy in Christ will cause the listener to desire the same experience.

By now it is no doubt easier to see the effective way in which the Holy Spirit works through musical style, talent and personality to lead others to a conversion experience. It must be remembered, however, that these do not constitute the fulfillment of the conversion, but rather serve as avenues which lead to the final step. The supreme test of the effectiveness of the tool is found in the ethical results obtained thereby.

4. *Music leads to conversion.* To convert is to turn around, or change one's course. When the listener has responded affirmatively to the message brought to him by the music, when he has been able to see beyond the messenger and the media, he is ready to receive the experience of conversion. "For every one that asketh receiveth; and he that seeketh findeth; and to him that knocketh it shall be opened" (Luke 11:10).

The work of redemption being complete, music fulfills two additional functions to the new believer in Christ:

a. It helps him recall the commitment he has made. "As ye have therefore received Christ Jesus the Lord, so walk ye in him" (Col. 2:6).

b. It challenges him to a deeper experience and a life of service. "I press toward the mark for the prize of the high calling of God in Christ Jesus" (Phil. 3:14).

In summary, the evangelistic ministry of music begins with the first perception of truth and is capable of carrying one through

to the fulfillment of the experience of redemption and on in the
Christian life.

Musical Trends in Evangelism

Ever since the singing of Paul and Silas was instrumental in
leading a jailer to the experience of salvation (Acts 16:25-31),
music has been a constant companion to evangelism. This is particularly to be noted in the study of some of the great evangelical
movements of the past four centuries. Even more noteworthy is
the vast difference in the style of music which was used in each of
these movements. For, just as the preaching had to be adapted to
meet the need of the particular era, so the music had to fulfill an
entirely new function as well. Space permits only a few outstanding examples of the needs that were felt during certain revival
eras and how they were met through music.

1. The Reformation (sixteenth century)

The needs: To cause man to return to the true teachings of
the Word of God; to present Christian doctrines in ways which
would be clearly understood by all men; to get the Word of God
into the hands of the people.

The implement used: Singing was restored to the possession
of the people on a large scale for the first time since the early years
of the Christian church, so that, in the words of Luther himself,
"God might speak directly to them in His Word and . . . they
might directly answer Him in their songs."[2] It was such an effective means of reaching hearts that Luther was accused by the
Roman opposition of overcoming the people with his songs.

2. The Wesleyan movement (eighteenth century)

The needs: To get men to return to a deeper relationship with
God; to present a gospel of personal challenge; to banish the religious sentimentalism that was prevalent in that day.

The implement used: Charles Wesley took many of the familiar
tunes of the day and set sacred texts to them, so that the people
would be attracted by the familiarity of the tunes and convicted
by the message of the texts. Those considered too sentimental were
eliminated by his brother John, including Charles's own "Jesus,
Lover of My Soul." John Wesley insisted that the congregational
singing be done with understanding, therefore he would frequently
stop the people in the middle of a song to remind them of the meaning of the words.

[2] E. S. Lorenz, *Practical Church Music* (New York: Fleming H. Revell Co.,
1909), p. 191.

3. The New England Revivals (middle eighteenth century)

The needs: To proclaim a message that would reach hearts; to place greater emphasis upon the grace of God.

The implement used: Because of the desire and need for personal music, Evangelist Jonathan Edwards introduced the hymns of Isaac Watts, the "father of English hymnody." Of this music Edwards testified, "There has been scarce any part of divine worship wherein good men among us have had grace so drawn forth, and their hearts so lifted in the ways of God, as in singing His praises."[3] So significant was the music during these revival efforts that the meetings became known as "singing meetings."

4. The camp meeting movements (early nineteenth century)

The need: To reach the people who possessed little or no education with a personal message of salvation in such a way as would be clearly understood by all.

The implement used: The gospel song, "a distinctly American phenomenon" which was "evangelical in spirit, but focused especially upon the winning of souls through conversion,"[4] was born in the camp meeting movements. While these songs were far from being literary masterpieces, they were so successful that the publication of a series of songbooks called *Gospel Hymns* resulted. This series of six editions was coedited by Philip P. Bliss and Ira D. Sankey, and "reached such popularity that, in some denominations, it even supplanted the authorized church hymnal."[5]

5. The Finney campaigns (middle nineteenth century)

The needs: To reach people who were not being affected by the work of the church; to win the "man of the street."

The implement used: In 1831, the Rev. Joshua Leavitt compiled a hymnal for use in these campaigns. This hymnal included secular tunes with sacred texts, which met great opposition from the church leaders. However, the songs were readily accepted by the people and greatly used in attracting and winning people for Christ.

6. The Moody revivals (late nineteenth century)

The needs: To provide a means of greater freedom in expression; to present the personal testimony of the believer in a unique and effective way.

The implement used: Distressed by the poor singing in his meet-

---

[3] Sellers, *op. cit.*, p. 109.

[4] A. E. Bailey, *The Gospel in Hymns* (New York: Charles Scribner's Sons, 1950), p. 482.

[5] E. E. Ryden, *The Story of Christian Hymnody* (Rock Island: Augustana Press, 1959), p. 557.

ings, Moody called on Ira D. Sankey to join him. Sankey's solos became so singularly used of God that Moody was said to have attributed 50 percent of the success of the campaigns to the singing. The Sankey songbook was published especially for use in the meetings, marking one of the initial steps toward a wide acceptance and usage of the gospel song.

7. The Sunday school movement in America (nineteenth century)

The needs: To reach children on their own levels of understanding; to teach the Word of God in simplicity and directness.

The implement used: New gospel songs were written for the movement by William Bradbury ("Saviour, Like a Shepherd Lead Us"), P. P. Bliss ("Jesus Loves Even Me"), Robert Lowry ("Nothing but the Blood") and others. These songs soon became known as "Sunday school songs."

8. The Billy Sunday meetings (early twentieth century)

The needs: To give expression to the emotional upheaval which was caused by the country's transition from a rural to an industrial society; to introduce an "energetic" type of singing and preaching which would attract and appeal to the unchurched.

The implement used: The singing was led by Homer Rodeheaver, a former college cheerleader. Under his leadership, a livelier type of gospel singing was introduced. The main emphasis in the singing was placed on songs of personal testimony. These were very effective and were instrumental in winning hundreds of men for Christ.

9. The Billy Graham campaigns

The needs: To reach a society which is culturally and socially minded; to appeal to the educated as well as the uneducated, to the leaders in governmental, religious and theatrical fields as well as to the laborer.

The implement used: This twentieth century revival movement under the leadership of Billy Graham has again witnessed the use of music as an implement of evangelism. Dr. Graham's team includes four musicians: a choir and congregational leader, a soloist, and two instrumentalists. Unlike the music used in the Billy Sunday meetings, the music in the Billy Graham meetings is a balance of hymns of praise and worship, standard gospel songs of personal testimony, and some new expressions of fellowship with Christ as penned by contemporary songwriters. The music has again served as a means of attracting the hearers and of expressing personal testimonies. But it has also been instrumental in drawing Christians closer to God and in winning others to Christ.

Music in Other Media of Evangelism

Church music has the power to reach people at all levels of understanding. In the words of Evangeline Booth, "It searches out every heart . . . it does not arouse argument, but the will to follow . . . it makes us remember all the good we have known and wish to find it again."[6] That is why its ministry is not limited to large evangelistic campaigns and church services. Some of the other areas of outreach to which music has effectively contributed are:

1. *On foreign soil.* Music is the universal language, and has proved its usefulness in many ways on the foreign mission field. For this reason, mission boards are now stressing the need for their candidates to have at least a basic amount of musical knowledge and, if possible, be able to play a portable instrument of some kind. Missionaries may use music in several ways.

a. As a means of initial contact. Music has often proved to be an open door through which missionaries have been able to find reception into the lives of the nationals, especially when they have been unable to communicate because of language barriers. A musical instrument is usually associated with good will, or is enough of a novelty to break down the feelings of strangeness.

b. As a means of attracting people. Instruments are also a great aid in assembling people, whether it be in attempting to conduct a street meeting in a metropolitan area in India, in trying to attract a wandering tribe of pygmies in Africa, or in seeking to reach a group of university students in Japan.

c. As a means of initial expression. Often music provides the missionary with a way to interpret and express that which he cannot say in a strange tongue. He is usually able to master a few good hymns or gospel songs in the native tongue long before he can speak the language fluently. Through the media of melody, harmony and rhythm, the nationals are able to ascertain the nature of the message clearly enough to know what is on the heart of the missionary, even when his command of the dialect is not perfect.

d. In the services. The missionary will frequently find opportunities to use his talents in providing special music, leading singing, directing choirs and instrumental groups. Contrary to the

[6] D. Nordin, *Quotes for Choirmasters* (Rock Island: Augustana Press, 1962). p. 10.

general concept of foreign missions, some missionaries work in churches which are equipped with organs, pianos and trained singers, and are accustomed to an active program of music.

Opportunities for musical missionaries. Not too many years ago, the full-time musical missionary was virtually unheard of. However, more opportunities are opening every year, and the number on the field keeps increasing as new needs arise. Some of the opportunities in missionary music are:

a. Radio and television. These media have become most useful in reaching tribes and individuals not normally touched by missionaries. Trained and experienced radio musicians, writers and technicians are needed to keep up this vital ministry.

b. Teaching music. Mission stations which maintain their own Bible schools or seminaries often want musicians to train song leaders, teach singing and direct choirs. Private lessons are always in demand for the children of the missionaries as well.

c. Translating and adapting words and music. Along with the rapid growth of radio and television ministries comes the increasing urgency to find people who are qualified to translate and adapt sacred music into the native tongues and musical styles. It is often more desirable to set sacred texts to familiar local tunes or chants. On the other hand, it is sometimes more advantageous to teach the American styles of gospel hymnody, translating some of these songs into the native tongues. This is especially necessary for tribes that have never associated their own music with anything but paganism or tribal wars.

2. *In rescue missions, hospitals and jails.* Some of the most rewarding ministries are to the down-and-outer, the physically impaired or the prisoner. This is true for at least three reasons:

a. He has little else to occupy his time, thus will listen to a message or a song.

b. He is greatly moved by the apparent interest and love shown by anyone who comes to minister.

c. He is often aware of a need in his life and wants help.

3. *Through radio, television, recordings and sacred films.* Although it is impossible to estimate the outreach these media have, it is a fact that they all rank high among the most effective implements of evangelism. Several reasons for this are:

a. They reach all people without regard to race, creed or social position.

b. They reach the people right where they are, in the homes, in automobiles, on the beach, or even in the tavern.

c. They are impersonal in their delivery, therefore tend to be disarming in their approach.

d. They are attractive in their manner of production, style and pacing.

e. They are usually relatively free from most church-associated "barriers."

4. *In youth camps.* This area of ministry, though equally effective, reaches people in a much different way than the media just mentioned. Personal contact is a major factor in youth camp work. Young people can be easily reached because the following conditions prevail:

a. They are usually required to attend services as part of the planned activities.

b. There is often a greater emphasis placed on serious things than usually found in the local church youth fellowship. Youth are encouraged to examine themselves carefully in programs of vocational guidance, athletic preparedness and spiritual emphasis.

c. An intimacy and informal relationship are usually developed between the youth and their counselors.

d. There is opportunity for active participation in music.

Reaching the Unchurched Through Music

There can be no stereotyping of musical styles, songs and approaches which are guaranteed to perform the ministry of evangelism. It is only through prayerful consideration and careful study that one can be assured of finding that music which is designed to meet the need of each particular situation. Perhaps the best way to begin is to analyze the many ways in which men can be reached for God, seeking to find one or more which may fit into the situation at hand. Some approaches which should be considered are:

1. Pointing out a person's need. It is a most difficult task to lead a man who is enjoying good health and prosperity to realize his need of a Saviour. That is why the well-to-do are frequently less receptive to the message than those in need of physical and temporal help. This type must be approached with a pertinent question such as found in the gospel song "Have You Any Room for Jesus?" (Whittle-Williams), or convinced of the true joy in Christ through such a testimony as presented in "Since I Have Been Redeemed" (Excell).

2. Offering a definite solution to the problem. He who knows he has a problem can be reached with a solution such as found

in "Look to the Lamb of God" (Jackson-Black) or "Jesus Never Fails" (A. A. Luther).

3. Giving a poignant reminder of the past. A song which recalls to mind a past association with the church or with godly parents or friends often reaches the heart more quickly and forcefully than any other means. Some of the old familiar songs may minister in this way.

4. Making an intellectual approach. The agnostic or the highly educated must often be reached through logic. In such cases the doctrinal hymns which are based on biblical facts, or those based on the elements of nature, will sometimes prove more influential than testimonies of personal experiences.

5. Giving a challenging approach. Youth are looking toward the future in hope of finding certainty and security. They will likely tend to respond to a gospel song such as "The Solid Rock" (Mote-Bradbury).

Common Misconceptions

The person who seeks to use music to win the lost for Christ will no doubt make many misjudgments concerning both the music he chooses and the people to whom he is ministering. Some of the common misconceptions which must be avoided are:

1. In the selection of music

a. Making communicability synonymous with simplicity. (If it is simple it will reach the heart; if it is difficult it must go over their heads.)

b. Making difficulty synonymous with quality. (If it is easy it is not good music; if it is hard it must be good music.)

c. Associating quality with musical style. (The gospel song is of low quality; the hymn is of high quality.)

d. Associating musical styles exclusively with types of ministries. (The gospel song is for evangelism; the hymn is for worship. Therefore, a gospel song should never be used in a worship service, nor a hymn in an evangelistic service.)

e. Linking tempi with spiritual effectiveness. (The lively songs inspire; the slow ones do not.)

These misconceptions are not entirely unfounded. They have been known to lead to dangerous generalities, such as are indicated above in parentheses.

2. In the evaluation of people

a. Don't assume that all down-and-outers are uneducated and

uncouth. Many narcotics and drug addicts roaming the streets today were once successful businessmen or women, often with good social and educational backgrounds.

b. Don't assume that all those of upper social status are well educated. Social registers contain the names of many people of very low intellect, often known as "mink coat illiterates," who have acquired status through marriage, inheritance or other means.

c. Don't think that all worldly-minded people will be attracted to Christ through sacred music of a popular style. Many will be driven away or will lose complete respect for the church if it has nothing higher to offer than the world has.

d. Don't think that all youth will be attracted by the "lively approach" to Christianity. Youth today is challenged by deep truths and profound thoughts, through debate teams, scholarship programs, school symphonies, concert choirs and private music lessons. He will be more apt to respond to a "religion" which confronts him with challenges and responsibilities as well as depth and quality.

A Positive Approach

Music chosen for evangelistic purposes should be communicable and yet above reproach. A positive approach to this choice should involve the following principles:

1. Choosing texts which will best convey the messages desired.

2. Choosing music that will best interpret and enhance the text, regardless of the style. The only other necessary point of consideration would be the level of difficulty in light of the ability of the one who is to perform it.

3. Performing as attractively as possible without drawing undue attention to the performer, except in the aspects necessary for communication.

Perhaps the best rules with which to conclude this study would be those which John Wesley set for his congregations: "Sing lustily; sing in time; above all, sing spiritually, with an eye to God in every word."[7] Finally, as a personal guide to assure a maximum of effectiveness, the performer might well ask himself the questions Wesley frequently asked his congregations: "Do you know what you said last? Did it suit your case? Did you sing it as to God, with the spirit and the understanding also?"[8]

[7] E. S. Lorenz, op. cit., p. 192.

[8] W. Douglas, Church Music in History and Practice (New York: Charles Scribner's Sons, 1937), p. 237.

RECOMMENDED READING

BLACKWOOD, A. W. *The Fine Art of Public Worship*. Nashville: Abingdon Press, 1934.

KERR, PHIL. *Music in Evangelism*. Glendale: Gospel Music Publishers, 1939.

LORENZ, E. S. *Practical Church Music*. New York: Fleming H. Revell Co., 1909.

LOVELACE, A. C., and RICE, W. C. *Music and Worship in the Church*. Nashville: Abingdon Press, 1960.

REYNOLDS, W. J. *A Survey of Christian Hymnody*. New York: Holt, Rinehart and Winston, Inc., 1963.

Chapter 5

STRUCTURE OF THE MUSIC
DEPARTMENT

Introduction

It is presumptuous to believe that all churches will have both a church music and a Christian education department. Yet it is safe to assume that most churches will conduct, or will be striving to develop, certain activities in these areas, if only on a small scale. Therefore, for the sake of clarity, we will in this chapter refer to the two departments whenever discussing any form of activity which would normally fall into the categories of music and Christian education.

No department is an entity in itself. It is only one vital part of a large operation and functions side by side with all other departments of the church. The goals of the church music department are basically the same as those of the department of Christian education, the ministry of visitation and all other phases of the overall church life. Although the techniques employed are somewhat different, each functions in the three areas of worship, Christian education, and evangelism.

Relationship to the Entire Church Program

The total ministry of the church is under the leadership of the pastor, who serves as the spiritual leader as well as the business administrator. It is his responsibility to oversee the work which takes place in each department, working closely with the church boards in legislating the church program, determining the equipment needed and the budget required for the year's operation. There are usually three divisions in the church board: one to care for the properties, equipment and finances; another to govern new policies, institute activities and select personnel; and the third to care for the spiritual problems of the membership, as well as to provide for the physical and temporal needs of the people.

ORGANIZATIONAL PLAN FOR THE CHURCH

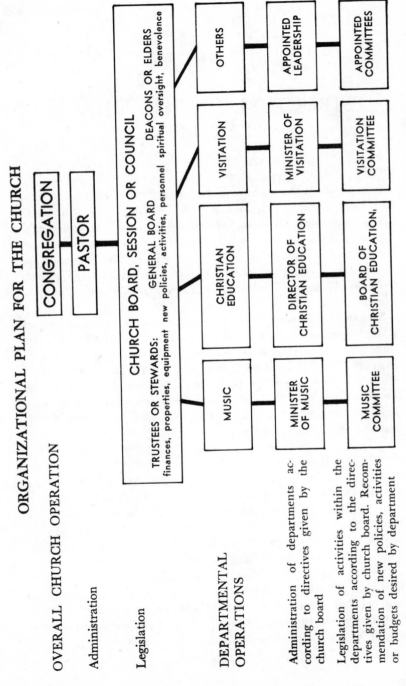

OVERALL CHURCH OPERATION

Administration

Legislation

CONGREGATION

PASTOR

CHURCH BOARD, SESSION OR COUNCIL

TRUSTEES OR STEWARDS: finances, properties, equipment

GENERAL BOARD new policies, activities, personnel

DEACONS OR ELDERS spiritual oversight, benevolence

MUSIC

CHRISTIAN EDUCATION

VISITATION

OTHERS

MINISTER OF MUSIC

DIRECTOR OF CHRISTIAN EDUCATION

MINISTER OF VISITATION

APPOINTED LEADERSHIP

MUSIC COMMITTEE

BOARD OF CHRISTIAN EDUCATION.

VISITATION COMMITTEE

APPOINTED COMMITTEES

DEPARTMENTAL OPERATIONS

Administration of departments according to directives given by the church board

Legislation of activities within the departments according to the directives given by church board. Recommendation of new policies, activities or budgets desired by department

The accompanying chart suggests the general organizational pattern followed in many churches. It is to be noted that there are two levels of activity, the overall church and the individual department. Each level has both administrative and legislative leadership. Therefore, the department director is the spiritual leader and administrator of his own area of work, and he cooperates with his own legislative board or committee in setting up departmental functions based on the directives given by the pastor and the church board.

The Operational Structure

The accompanying chart shows the final division of the overall structure of the individual departments, the operational division. This division includes all the active groups or functions which make up the departmental program. In the church music department this includes the choirs, instrumental ensembles and music classes.

The program of operation may vary in size from one choir to a complete program such as has been outlined on the chart. Regardless of its simplicity or complexity, the method of operation will be the same. Following are suggestions of some ways in which the program may be set up.

1. Graded choir program. Ideally, the structure of a graded choir system will correspond with the Sunday school, which usually correlates either with the public school grades or with the ages of the children.

FULL GRADED CHOIR PROGRAM

Preschool	ages 3 - 5		
Primary	ages 6 - 8	or	grades 1 - 3
Junior	ages 9 - 11	or	grades 4 - 6
Junior high	ages 12 - 14	or	grades 7 - 9
High school	ages 15 - 17	or	grades 10 - 12
College age	ages 18 - 22		
Adult	ages 23 and above		

It is often advisable to alter the structure to correspond with any unusual variance in either the public school or the Sunday school. For example, if the local school system does not have a junior high school, the following alternate plan could be used:

COMPACT GRADED CHOIR PROGRAM

Preschool	ages 3 - 5		
Elementary	ages 6 - 9	or	grades 1 - 4
Intermediate	ages 10 - 13	or	grades 5 - 8
Youth	ages 14 - 17	or	grades 9 - 12
College age and/or adult	ages 18 and above		

In either of these programs, the preschool choir may be omitted and the adult and college-age groups may be either separate or combined. Size of each choir and availability of leadership are always important factors in developing a choir program. If the potential is great enough, it would be wise to add both a men's and a women's chorus; or the children's choirs, particularly the junior high, could be divided into boys' and girls' choruses.

A more practical program for the small church would be the following:

SMALL GRADED CHOIR PROGRAM

Junior	ages 7 - 11	or	grades 2 - 6
Youth	ages 12 - 15	or	grades 7 - 10
Adult	ages 16 and above		

The wider span of ages in each group may present a few new problems, none of which should be insurmountable. The fact that each choir is larger will more than compensate for these problems.

2. Music classes. Perhaps there are no fixed ways of organizing and conducting classes in a church music program. Many systems incorporate enough training into the choirs and instrumental groups to make extra classes unnecessary. Others incorporate classroom instruction into the Christian education and youth programs as discussed in the chapter on "Music in Christian Education." Even the types of classes considered would be designed to meet specific needs in the church, such as sightsinging for new choir members, hymn playing for departmental pianists and accompanists, or conducting for Sunday school leaders.

3. Instrumental ensembles. These should be built around the instrumentation found in the church membership. Several possible plans of organization are suggested in the chapter on "Instrumental Ensembles," each based on the principle of distributing the available instrumentalists in the most practical way possible, so that all will have opportunity to participate.

MUSIC DEPARTMENT

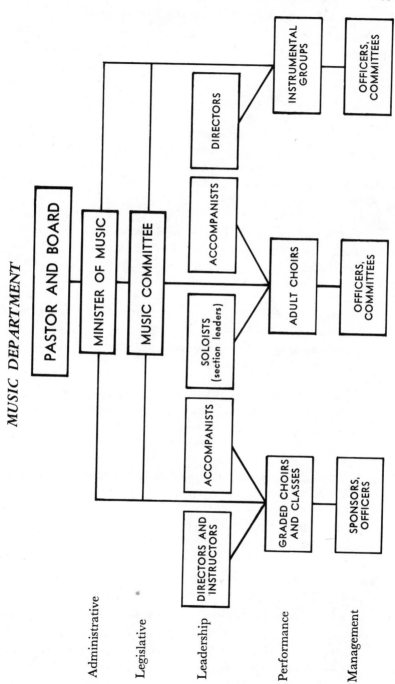

Management Groups Within the Department

It is to be noted on the departmental chart that each musical organization has a management group to handle the many affairs which are directly related to that organization alone.

Lay leadership is a necessary part of each of the musical groups. In the children's choirs and ensembles, this would be in the form of sponsors (usually mothers or fathers of the children), with only a limited emphasis on leadership from the children themselves. In the youth groups, greater responsibilities would be given to the officers, but the main part of the lay leadership would still come from adult sponsors (at this age, young married couples are preferred). The adult groups would .have active, functional officers from their own ranks.

1. The sponsors. The sponsors hold no position of authority, except in the management of the activities in their group. They are appointed by the music committee, and some of them will be delegated to serve as representatives to the committee. Their responsibilities vary according to the age with which they work, but include the following:

a. Attending all rehearsals and choir appearances.

b. Keeping attendance records and cooperating with the departmental secretary in maintaining charts of progress and achievements.

c. Sending out absentee cards and other announcements.

d. Handling necessary discipline problems during rehearsals.

e. Caring for robes and vestments.

f. Providing assistance in drill sessions when necessary.

g. Assisting with processionals and lining up before services.

h. Helping in the planning of socials and refreshment breaks during rehearsals.

i. Recruiting new members.

2. The officers. The officers and committees of the adult groups function in particular areas:

a. Assisting the director in much of the detail work mentioned above.

b. Providing a contact between the congregation and the choir.

c. Serving as a liaison between the director and the choir members.

The number of officers and committees needed depends upon the extent of the activities carried on by the group. Although suggested responsibilities may vary, the following are essential to any adult group:

President, who shall take charge of business meetings, see that all duties are performed by officers and committees, make appointments of nonelective positions, keep the members informed of forthcoming activities.

Vice-president, who shall preside at business meetings in the absence of the president, assume the presidency in event of a vacancy between elections, serve as chairman of the membership committee.

Secretary, who shall keep a record of attendances, keep the director informed of ineligibilities due to excess absence, handle any correspondence necessary.

Treasurer, who shall be responsible for handling funds, paying bills, taking up the weekly collection (if any) during rehearsal.

Librarian, who shall be responsible for distributing and collecting music at rehearsals and services, marking, filing and repairing music, ordering and maintaining periodicals and books in the lending library.

Robe committee, which shall be responsible for assigning robes, collars and/or vestments, making arrangements for their cleaning, repairing and replacing when necessary.

Social committee, which shall plan and arrange all social functions of the group, including the entertainment of visiting musical groups.

Membership committee, which shall plan and conduct periodic membership programs or drives, seek out new prospects and inform the director, seek to improve relationships among present members.

Other suggested committees include publicity, properties and nominating committees. Other suggested officers include a chaplain, representative to the music committee, correspondence secretary, and assistant librarian as needed.

Legislative Group: the Music Committee

The music committee should be a well-balanced representation of all the musical organizations and leaders, plus the pastor, director of Christian education, and representatives from the boards and the general membership of the church. Its organizational structure may look like the following:

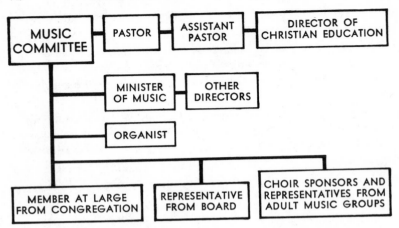

Meetings of the committee should be scheduled quarterly, unless pressure of business demands more frequent sessions.

Functions. The value of a music committee has been frequently contested. Though there are definite legislative responsibilities which must be fulfilled in the department, the extent of the authority given this committee is sometimes very limited, and its duties are of such a nature as to require little or no activity. On the other hand, there will be times when it will have to make many vital decisions. Its responsibilities will be as follows:

1. Active responsibilities. The committee is authorized to appoint all nonsalaried assistants in the department, including choir mothers, sponsors, department secretaries, accompanists and assistant directors.

2. Intermediary responsibilities. It has the power of recommending appointments of new salaried personnel, salary changes, budget changes, purchase of equipment not provided for in the budget, or changes in the program of the department. If special designation of authority has been given to act upon the above details rather than simply recommend, all actions must be made in concurrence with the programs, policies and budgets established by the church board.

3. Advisory responsibilities. As a representation of the people, the committee is delegated to inform the leadership of any pertinent suggestions or expressions of commendation or dissatisfaction coming from the members of the music groups, boards or congregation. Although this does not constitute the making of rules or recommending of policies, it helps to clarify present goals and thereby lead to future changes or improvements in the program.

4. Emergency responsibilities. In the event of situations which demand immediate action, the committee is authorized to appoint temporary personnel, or to assume any responsibilities which cannot be fulfilled by members of the music staff, until such time as it is possible to make permanent arrangements.

Administrative Assistant

In a large musical organization it is advisable to appoint a departmental secretary to assist the minister of music in coordinating activities, and to work with the individual choir sponsors in keeping records. This position can be a voluntary or part-time office occupied by a church member, or the assignment of a secretary already employed in the church or Christian education department.

The primary responsibility is that of keeping attendance records and project charts on all members of the music groups and classes. Through this means the progress and achievement of each child and adult can be followed throughout his entire choir career, and a program of awards can be administered on a departmental basis. A special ledger should be maintained for each group and a separate file card for each member. Achievements recorded should include:

1. Perfect attendance, or accumulation of points for good attendance.
2. Fulfillment of musical goals set forth by the choir, and/or completion of assigned workbooks or projects.
3. Bringing new members to choir (or any of the choirs).
4. Hymn memorization, as designated by the department.
5. Scripture memorization, as designated by the department.
6. Engagement in extracurricular activities, such as music and poetry writing contests and performing in recitals.

RECOMMENDED READING

ASHTON, J. N. *Music in Worship*. Boston: Pilgrim Press, 1943.

NININGER, RUTH. *Growing a Musical Church*. Nashville: Broadman Press, 1947.

WILSON, H. R. and LYALL, J. L. *Building a Church Choir*. Minneapolis: Hall and McCreary Company, 1957.

Chapter 6

ADMINISTRATIVE LEADERSHIP

Introduction

As will be seen throughout the following study, the leaders of the music program in the Old Testament temples, under David, Solomon, and later Ezra, were expected to be spiritual leaders as well as skilled musicians. "These are they whom David set over the service of song in the house of the Lord" (I Chron. 6:31). The structure of the music program was in many ways similar to that suggested in the preceding chapter, with the king himself maintaining administrative leadership and each leader delegated to train in the various instruments as well as singing, finally preparing his group for use in public worship.

According to I Chronicles 15, the program of leadership was constructed somewhat as follows:

```
              ┌─────────────────────────────┐
              │   DAVID: administrator       │
              │   (I Chron. 15:16; 16:4)     │
              └─────────────────────────────┘

              ┌─────────────────────────────┐
              │   CHENANIAH: leader of song  │
              │      (I Chron. 15:22)        │
              └─────────────────────────────┘

┌──────────────┐   ┌──────────────┐   ┌──────────────┐
│    HEMAN     │   │    ASAPH     │   │    ETHAN     │
└──────────────┘   └──────────────┘   └──────────────┘
```

Singers, instrumentalists (I Chron. 15:16, 17, 19)
Instructors (I Chron. 25:1-7)
Leaders with cymbals (I Chron. 16:5, 41, 42)

Qualifications, challenges and duties which accompany each of the positions of leadership in a present-day church music ministry will be discussed, including those of the pastor, the minister of music, and all who are given responsibilities of leadership.

The Pastor

Good pastoral leadership is an absolute determining factor in the success of a church music program. The pastor cannot assume an attitude of unconcern toward the music program, since it involves so much of the total ministry of his church. The effectiveness of the music ministry will influence the effectiveness of the entire church ministry.

Under normal circumstances, the pastor should not be charged with the task of personally conducting the music program. However, the extent of his responsibilities is often determined by the number of staff employed or the number of qualified laymen available to do the work. The pastor of one church may be expected to attend to all the music, Christian education, youth work, visitation and office responsibilities, whereas another may have little or no direct obligations to these areas. In either case, his position as spiritual leader and church administrator brings him into direct contact with the activities of these departments.

There are six specific ways in which the pastor of the church should function in the music program.

1. The pastor oversees the work of the music department. In the temple music program, David appointed musicians to minister "over the service of song in the house of the Lord" (I Chron. 6:31). Although he himself was a musician, he placed the trust of leadership, training, and performance in the hands of a staff of skilled personnel (15:16), but continued as administrator over the work by assigning particular responsibilities to each (25:1) and seeing that they were fulfilled.

It is often difficult to discern between operational and administrative leadership. The pastor must be certain that he does not interpose himself in the program in such a way that he limits the effectiveness of the minister of music and his associates. On the other hand, the outcome of the activities in the department is his direct responsibility; therefore he must be certain that all the duties are properly discharged and that the attainments are worthwhile.

2. The pastor seeks to understand and appreciate the music program. Ideally, the pastor will have training and background in music, will have developed a sound philosophy concerning the ministry of music, and will understand the general structure of a church music program. Unfortunately, the seminary curriculum does not prepare him sufficiently in these fields; therefore he must often encounter the problems without proper preparation. When this is true, he should attend music workshops and read good literature on church music and hymnology in an effort to develop knowledge in these fields.

He should also be willing to accept new ideas and occasional experimental programs when suggested by the minister of music.

3. The pastor confides in the music leadership. A good working relationship between pastor and musicians requires mutual confidence and accord in understanding how music ministers and communicates. The pastor should display genuine trust in the decisions made by those who are chosen to responsible positions in the department. Except for instances when their decisions are obviously indiscreet, those holding leadership responsibility in the music program should be given full authority to select materials, determine rehearsal procedures and techniques, and plan the contents of special musical programs and service music.

4. The pastor assists in the planning. He should meet frequently with the music leaders to help plan the musical program as it relates to the public services of the church, and to discuss their areas of work. He should not only offer ideas and suggestions but also seek their counsel on matters pertaining to the musical life of the church, basing his decisions on their mutual agreements.

5. The pastor arbitrates in the music problems. Most of the problems which might occur in the music department will be prevented by the previously mentioned planning sessions. But there are times when the pastor must become an arbitrator between the leaders and the participants, the congregation or the board. Intervention is particularly necessary when there is evidence of:

a. Disregard for policies, budgets and directives.

b. Unwise selection of texts which are not biblically founded.

c. Controversy in one or more of the musical groups.

d. Spiritual decline in the department.

6. The pastor undergirds the music program with prayer and encouragement. The most important contribution the pastor can make is a personal interest in the music program. A sincere interest will be revealed in the following ways:

a. By praying, both privately and publicly, for its ministries, its leaders and its members.

b. By commending and encouraging when progress has been made or when a task has been well performed.

c. By attending an occasional rehearsal or social function.

d. By acknowledging his dependence upon the music program.

Conclusion. In many churches, the choice of hymns for the worship services is the responsibility of the pastor. There are many obvious advantages to his assuming this task, the primary one being that he is conscious of the theme which should be followed through the service. Hs is, however, at a distinct disadvantage if he has not studied hymnology or does not know music well enough to determine whether or not the style, tempo and mood idea will adapt to the part of the service desired. It is advisable that the choice of hymns be a combined effort of both the minister of music and the pastor, or that periodically they confer and discuss the hymns to be used.

The pastor is, in the final analysis, the most important person in the church music program, for "its level cannot rise higher than his estimation of its importance in the life of the church."[1]

The Minister of Music

The title minister of music is a general form of address ascribed to the person charged with the responsibility of officiating over the music program of the church.

How he may function. He may function in one of the following ways:

1. Full-time director of music—one who devotes his full time to the specific ministry of:

a. Organizing and directing the church music program.

b. Conducting the choirs and instrumental groups, and teaching music classes.

c. Assisting the pastor in the planning of the church services, concerts and special programs in which music is a vital part.

d. Training and developing talent within the church membership.

e. Visiting and counseling members of the music groups—and their families—in times of need.

f. Recruiting new members for the music groups.

The director of music is assisted by at least one person, the church organist, but will often employ the services of other musicians or laymen as accompanists, conductors of various choral and instrumental groups, or congregational song leaders. This being the case, he assumes supervisory responsibility over them.

2. Organist-choirmaster—one who, in addition to the duties set forth for the director of music, also plays the organ and accompanies rehearsals. Due to his additional obligations, he may rely even more upon the assistance of other accompanists, conductors and song leaders to facilitate his music program.

His effectiveness as a combined director-accompanist depends largely on his ability to communicate with the choir while per-

[1] A. C. Lovelace and W. C. Rice, *Music and Worship in the Church* (Nashville: Abingdon Press, 1960), p. 41.

forming adequately at the console. This is a complex task which usually takes years of training in both conducting and accompanying. It also calls for a proper arrangement of choir loft and organ console so that he can be seen by all members of the choir, either directly or through a mirror. If the general construction of the sanctuary prohibits this, he should employ an assistant accompanist or director.

3. *Christian education-music director*—one who is responsible for both the music and the Christian education work of the church. This combination is found frequently in the medium-sized church of three hundred to six hundred active members, where neither department has grown to the extent that it needs the services of a full-time director, or where the budget of the church does not permit two full-time directors. His duties in the area of music will be similar to those previously mentioned, but will not be as extensive because of the added responsibilities of Christian education. He would probably depend upon professional or lay assistance in both areas, and would then assume a greater degree of administrative obligation over the two departments.

The Christian education-music director must be well trained in both fields and must have an equal interest in each. If not, there will be a tendency to neglect one in favor of the other. The church schedule must also be carefully planned so as to avoid any overlapping of activities, which would again present similar problems of neglect. If the above conditions are met, he can have an effective, fruitful ministry in both areas.

4. *Part-time director of music or organist-choirmaster*—one who is devoting his spare time to the ministry of music while engaged in a profession or occupation outside the church. He may be a professional musician, private or school music teacher, or a layman who considers music his most effective means of service to the Lord. He may be giving his time voluntarily or receiving a small remuneration for his services. His duties will be similar to those previously listed for the minister of music, but will be limited to the time he can spend. Perhaps the music program will not be large, yet it may be ample for the size of the church. If, however, the church program calls for a more extensive ministry than one part-time person can manage, it will be beneficial to employ more than one part-time music director. In this type of arrangement, one should assume the position of minister of music, with the others working as his associates. If this plan does not work, the pastor

should serve actively as administrator of the music department, giving each of the musicians clearly defined areas in which to work.

Five aspects of the music director's ministry. The dictionary defines a minister as "one subordinate to another; one entrusted with the direction of affairs; a servant; an agent; an ambassador." These five points clearly describe the diverse aspects found in the position of minister of music.

1. He is a subordinate. "Obey them that have the rule over you, and submit yourselves" (Heb. 13:17). In much the same manner as the departmental supervisor in a large corporation, the minister of music must work under the direction of the pastor. It is his task to develop a program which will not be competitive to any other area of the church work, but which will contribute to the complete program as outlined by the church board and administered by the pastor. Although he is given authority in certain areas, he must learn to experience disappointment when his ideas are rejected, and must learn never to step ahead of the wishes of the pastor or church board.

2. He is a leader. "He counted me faithful, putting me into the ministry" (I Tim. 1:12). The trust of administration of musical affairs has been placed upon him. Within the framework which has been set up by the board, he is authorized to plan programs, choose music and determine policies, as well as to give directives to those working with him in the department.

3. He is a servant. "I am among you as he that serveth" (Luke 22:27). Even as Jesus Christ considered himself a servant to the people whom He came to ransom, the minister of music is to be subservient to the members of his musical groups, seeking to fulfill their musical and spiritual needs. He must minister regularly to their needs of training, inspiration and encouragement in the rehearsals. However, his work extends into the areas of personal needs as well, and he must be prepared to give help in any way possible.

4. He is an agent. "Declare his glory among the heathen, his wonders among all people" (Ps. 96:3). As an agent, he has a threefold responsibility:

a. To the author. His primary responsibility is to the message of the text. He must see to it that this is given the proper interpretation, that the choir members "sing with the spirit, and . . . with the understanding also" (I Cor. 14:15).

b. To the composer. The musical intentions of the composer

must be carefully studied so that the correct dynamics, tempi, phrases and moods are projected into the performance.

c. To the congregation. His obligation to the message (the text) and the method of propagating it (the music) is not finalized until it reaches the recipient (the congregation). It is the responsibility of the minister of music to see that nothing in the performance will stand in the way of a clear presentation of the message, that nothing within the message will deter from the sacred truths of the Word of God, and that nothing within the music will conceal the true meaning within the text.

5. *He is an ambassador*. "Now then we are ambassadors for Christ" (II Cor. 5:20). The dictionary defines an ambassador as "an accredited representative . . . charged with a special mission." The minister of music must be personally acquainted with the One whom he represents. In all that he does—as he works with the pastor and board in the total church program, as he directs the activities of his own department, as he serves the members of his music groups, and as he seeks to translate notes and words into a message that will reach hearts—he must thereby be an ambassador for Christ. His charge as an ambassador is well defined in the words of Charles Wesley, one of the greatest ministers of music that ever lived:

> To serve the present age,
>   My calling to fulfill;
> Oh, may it all my powers engage
>   To do my Master's will.

Musical requirements. "Chenaniah, chief of the Levites, was for song: he instructed about the song, because he was skilful" (I Chron. 15:22). This person, selected by David to be the master of song in the temple, was chosen largely because of his skill in performance as well as in teaching. The minister of music must possess musical abilities that distinguish him from the other lay musicians with whom he works. His skills are necessary not only for the tasks which he has to perform but also to command the respect and authority which he must have in his position of leadership. The vital musical requirements needed are:

1. Basic requirements.

a. Conducting ability

b. Sight-reading ability

c. A good ear for pitch perception and tone

d. Innate musicianship, which includes the "feeling" of rhythms, phrases and harmonic sequences

e. Thorough understanding of music theory

f. Knowledge of the essentials of vocal production

g. At least a minimum of piano proficiency

h. An understanding of organ stop registrations, if not organ proficiency

i. A well-rounded repertoire of vocal, choral and instrumental music, especially in the areas in which he is actively participating

2. Performance requirements. The specific performance requirements of the minister of music depend largely on his area of active responsibilities, either as soloist, organist, accompanist or director. Each of these is considered separately in the next chapter. It must be observed that his capabilities as a director and an administrator are greatly affected by his experience and ability as a performer, whether or not he uses his performance skills in his work.

3. Additional desirable skills. In addition to the skills of conducting and performing, he should be equipped to do any of the following:

a. Arrange or adapt music. With a basic knowledge of how to arrange, he can supply his choirs, vocal ensembles and instrumentalists with many interesting and useful hymn settings or accompaniments. In working with children's choirs, this is especially useful for adapting music to their vocal ranges and music limitations. It is also essential to be able to transpose instrumental parts and to adapt music to the many instrumental combinations which may be available.

b. Supply repertoire and technical help for aspiring instrumental and vocal soloists. A large part of his ministry should be that of training and helping young musicians. In so doing, he is not only doing a service to the individuals but also assuring himself of future soloists, accompanists and qualified assistants.

Imperatives for leadership. The title minister implies the following imperatives:

1. Dedication. According to the command of David, sanctification was a prerequisite to the fulfilling of any responsibility in the house of God. The Levites who were appointed over the "tabernacle of testimony" to "minister unto it" (Num. 1:50) were commanded to sanctify themselves (I Chron. 15:12). It was after this act was fulfilled that David "spake to the chief of the Levites to appoint their brethren to be the singers with instruments of musick, psalteries and harps and cymbals, sounding, by lifting up the voice with joy" (v. 16). Chenaniah, chief of the Levites, was appointed the "master of the song" (v. 27), with Heman, Asaph and Ethan assisting him with the instruments (vv. 17-21).

The basic spiritual requirements for the leader in music are that he:

a. Experience redemption and forgiveness of sins (Eph. 1:7). No person can expect to have a ministry of any value at all unless he is personally committed to the One whom he serves.

b. Feel the call of God to serve (Eph. 3:7, 8). His work cannot be looked upon as a mere musical profession or artistic expression, nor can it be entered into for the sake of personal gain. It must be thought of as an opportunity and a responsibility to serve God.

c. Dedicate his life, time and talents to the task to which he has been called. The Apostle Paul clearly set forth the principle of dedication when he wrote these words to the church at Rome: "I beseech you therefore, brethren, by the mercies of God, that ye present your bodies a living sacrifice, holy, acceptable unto God, which is your reasonable service" (Rom. 12:1). Through this act of dedication he will receive the power of the Holy Spirit needed to fulfill his obligations as a minister of the gospel through music.

2. Musicianship. Musical ability was also an important consideration in the selecting of temple musicians. Chenaniah was appointed "because he was skilful" (I Chron. 15:22).

The three basic essentials of good musicianship are:

a. An innate musical ability

b. Consistent practice

c. Continuous development in the techniques

The temple musicians devoted their entire lives to training and developing their own talents, as well as assisting in the development of the skills of others, "for they were employed in that work day and night" (I Chron. 9:33). This does not mean that an amateur church musician, one who has only a limited amount of training, ability and time to spare, cannot have a successful ministry. Many churches depend on this type of leadership and, with the help of the Lord, are able to maintain a fruitful ministry in music. However, it is important for this leader to realize his limitations and to strive for continued improvement.

Even the highly skilled musician must continue to practice. Good performances depend more on rehearsal than skill. He must also be on a constant search for new materials, expanded repertoire and improved methods. Fresh approaches are stimulating to rehearsals and usually will result in improved performances.

Whereas this pursuit for continued development can be best realized through professional study, it can also be found in home study, in reading related books and periodicals, in perusing materials found in music stores and libraries, in attending church music workshops, and in joining church music fellowships, which seek to give help to the church musician.

3. *Knowledge of the teachings of the Bible.* David's command to his musicians was to "sing unto him, sing psalms unto him, talk ye of all his wondrous works" (I Chron. 16:9), to "show forth from day to day his salvation" (v. 23). The Apostle Paul adds to it the charge which should apply to all ministers of the Word of God: "a workman that needeth not to be ashamed, rightly dividing the word of truth" (II Tim. 2:15). The church musician "divides the word of truth" in three ways:

a. By the manner in which he selects and interprets music. In selecting music, he must be able to determine whether or not the text is in accord with Bible doctrines. This requires a good understanding of theology as well as a thorough knowledge of the Bible. If the text is based on portions of Scripture, he must be able to discern between that which has been drawn out of its proper context and that which propounds the truth in the manner originally intended. Finally he must know whether or not the music adequately interprets the full meaning of the text. An interpreter of the music, he must also be an expositor of the message within.

b. By the manner in which he conducts himself. His standard of living, business practices, moral and ethical life, and his attitude toward others all indicate whether or not he embraces the teachings of the Word of God himself. "Whoso keepeth his word, in him verily is the love of God perfected: hereby know we that we are in him. He that saith he abideth in him ought himself also so to walk, even as he walked" (I John 2:5, 6).

c. By the manner in which he deals with his fellow workers. Part of the ministry of leadership involves the personal encountering of spiritual and temporal needs. The church musician must be able to administer words of comfort, assurance, challenge and even chastening to the lay musicians with whom he works. Many of them look up to him as their pastor and counselor, therefore he must be able to show them through the Word of God the way of salvation, the work of the Holy Spirit, the doctrines of the church and those things which pertain to their Christian life and ministry.

4. *Understanding of the beliefs and practices of the local church.* The church musician should never agree to engage himself in the

music program of a church unless he is able to give wholehearted support to the teaching of the church. On the other hand, there may be minor practices or principles with which he may not fully agree, many of which will not affect his ministry or his relationship with the people. He must understand these differences and thereby determine the degree of variance between these and his own beliefs. There are at least four areas in which many Bible-believing churches may differ without altering their basic beliefs in the doctrines of the Bible.

a. In the ordinances observed. Several modes of baptism, infant dedication, confirmation and ordination are practiced in churches today, and the degree of importance placed upon these things varies greatly.

b. In the order of service used. Perhaps the greatest variances lie between liturgical and free-type worship practices, yet even the liturgies differ among denominations and individual churches. Some churches place great importance upon the use of responses, litanies and other forms of participation, while others consider these detrimental to the true spirit of free worship.

c. The doctrinal positions held. Bible-believing churches hold several doctrinal positions on subjects such as the millennium, the person and work of the Holy Spirit, the security of believers and the like. When these particular positions are not contrary to the basic message of salvation, the Spirit-filled life and the assurance of life after death, it is possible for the church musician to enjoy an effective ministry and warm relationship even when these beliefs differ slightly from his own.

d. The traditions practiced. Innumerable customs have been carried into church worship as a result of cherished practices in other countries. It is important that the church musician honor these and cooperate in their usage. If he is given opportunity to change these patterns of practice, he should do so with discretion, seeking only to improve the effectiveness of the overall program of worship without offending.

5. *Adaptability to the cultural level of the congregation.* It would be exceedingly difficult for the church musician to perform an effective ministry in any church wherein his cultural level is far removed, either above or below the members of the congregation. The basic cultural traditions and aptitudes of the church members will have great influence on their personal acceptance or rejection of the music program he offers them. The kind of music they have been accustomed to hearing in their church over a period of

years cannot help but affect their level of understanding and tastes. The church musician must therefore adapt himself and his music program to meet the demands enforced upon him by the culture and background of the people with whom he is to serve.

6. *Love for people.* One of the most sensitive aspects of the ministry is that of dealing with personalities. The Christian leader is frequently faced with the problem of having to adjust his plans and alter his program to satisfy the demands of the temperamental member of a board or committee. He must have a genuine love for people to tolerate many of these occurrences. He must know how to be a diplomat among the undiplomatic, to be tolerant when others are intolerant, to be patient with the impatient, and to be loving when others are most unloving. "Seeing we have this ministry, as we have received mercy, we faint not" (II Cor. 4:1). "If God so loved us, we ought also to love one another" (I John 4:11).

RECOMMENDED READING

The Pastor:

BLACKWOOD, A. W. *The Fine Art of Public Worship.* Nashville: Abingdon Press, 1934.

HALTER, CARL. *The Practice of Sacred Music.* St. Louis: Concordia Publishing House, 1955.

SYDNOR, J. R. *Planning for Church Music.* Nashville: Abingdon Press, 1961.

The Minister of Music:

BACON, ALLAN. *The True Function of Church Music.* Stockton, Calif.: Printwell Press, 1953.

LOVELACE, A. C., and RICE, W. C. *Music and Worship in the Church.* Nashville: Abingdon Press, 1960.

WILSON, H. R., and LYALL, J. L. *Building a Church Choir.* Minneapolis: Hall and McCreary Company, 1957.

Chapter 7

OTHER LEADERSHIP

It has already been established that the music program, while under the administration of the pastor and the minister of music, is dependent upon many people to keep it functioning. The previous chapter made mention of the five imperatives necessary for all those considered to be leaders and performers of music in the church. This chapter is devoted to the individual responsibilities which each of these holds in his own specific area as director, instrumentalist and soloist.

The Music Director or Instructor

The director is the one most responsible for a music group, whether it be a class, a choir, an instrumental ensemble, or the congregational "choir" as it sings its hymns under his direction.

1. His responsibilities

Whether or not the directorship is handled by the minister of music alone, the responsibilities of each group director are similar to the previously mentioned five aspects of the former's ministry. The director of one music group within a large department is subordinate to those in authority over him; he is also a leader of his own group, a servant to its membership, an agent of the message contained in the music, and an ambassador for Christ.

2. Specific knowledge necessary

a. Conducting ability. The ability to conduct is not limited to the knowledge of basic patterns, preparatory beats, releases and fermatas. As important as they may be, they are ineffective unless they are properly coordinated with the spirit of the music. Sateren suggests, "Match your beat with the type of tone you want."[1] The simplest approach to expressive conducting is to adjust the size of the beat, its level (high, medium or low), its speed and its intensity to the tempo, mood and dynamics of the music. A proper coordination will result in new feelings of expression in the beat.

---

[1] L. B. Sateren, *The Good Choir* (Minneapolis: Augsburg Publishing House, 1963), p. 5.

Expressive conducting, however, is not limited to the beat alone; it is a skillful blending of all the component parts of the director's body.

His eyes interpret the moods and feelings.

His mouth assists in the proper pronunciation of the words.

His hands indicate the amount of intensity desired.

His wrists suggest degrees of strength or flexibility.

His body commands forthrightness, caution or confidence.

Each of these parts of the body must be studied as to its relation to the conducting beat.

b. Comprehension of the music. Each individual composition must be studied carefully so that the following may be understood:

The style of the music

The themes and recurrent devices used by the composer

The relationship between the music and the text

The overall picture as well as the small thoughts contained therein

The interpretation of music involves the treatment of both the general ideas and the intricate thoughts. The director must be able to read in, as well as between, the lines.

c. Concept of the need. Robert Shaw suggests that "a director's ears are more important than his arms."[2] In order to fulfill the demands of the music, he must be able to hear what is wrong and know what needs to be corrected. It takes a well-trained ear to hear blend, pitch, intonation, balance and tone. Yet an ear for all of these is vital if the effectiveness of the choir is going to be improved.

d. Command of musical techniques. Skillful conducting requires both an inherent and an immediate command of music. The director's approach to the choir should be that of building musicianship and developing good vocal production through everything he does in the rehearsal. His approach to instrumental groups should be similar, involving good tone production as it pertains to the particular instruments. This obviously requires training in the techniques of voice and instruments, plus good musicianship. However, it is not sufficient for him to have knowledge and ability unless he also has developed methods through which he can successfully impart these techniques to his group.

e. Control over people. It is possible to meet all these requirements yet still not be able to get the desired results from the group.

---

[2] D. W. Nordin, *Quotes for Choirmasters* (Rock Island, Ill.: Augustana Press. 1962), p. 17.

This may possibly be due to inability to communicate. The true secret of communication lies in his ability to command—not demand—their respect, and to control—not compel—a response. Members will often achieve high goals because of their respect for and response to the director, but seldom in spite of him. He must help them:

See what must be done and how it may be accomplished.

Understand the spiritual and musical values in the accomplishment.

Become enthusiastic toward the fulfilling of the task.

f. Consciousness of the group's limitations. The composer Robert Schumann once said, "Try to perform simple pieces well and perfectly. It is better than to perform difficult ones badly." The choice of music should be largely determined by the following:

Age of the group members

Size of the group and balance of parts

Musical ability and experience

Rehearsal time available

Ability of the conductor and accompanist

g. Challenge to the group's potential. The knowledge of the limitations may restrict, but it also opens new avenues for improvement. Consequently, the present limitations can become the goals for future achievement. The genuine optimism of the director, plus an organized program of achievements desired, can result in almost limitless developments.

3. Special qualifications

There are certain qualities which tend to make one director more suited to one age group than another. They include:

a. His love for the particular age

b. His understanding of their emotional characteristics

c. His awareness of their potential in musicianship, vocal techniques and spiritual development

d. His ability to adapt his teaching approaches to their level

e. His knowledge of how this group fits into the total musical program

f. His capability of winning their respect and response

The Organist

Whether it is a part-time, full-time or voluntary position, the organist's responsibilities may be structured three ways: (1) As a combined organist-choirmaster, in which organization and leadership are added to the organ responsibilities. (2) As regular church organist, in which position he is working with the director of music, yet personally accountable for the playing of the entire service, accompanying, and supplying preludes, offertories and postludes. (3) As rehearsal accompanist, or organist for a special group, in which his duties are restricted to certain areas assigned him by the minister of music.

1. Ministry of the organist

a. In leadership. In the Old Testament, the accompanying instruments were the leaders of the singing of the choirs. The musical directors led with the cymbals, and the priests sounded the pitches with the trumpets (II Chron. 5:12,13; Ezra 3:10,11). Every organist must assume a certain degree of responsibility for making decisions and controlling of performances. This is especially true when he is accompanying the congregation, since he is functional in establishing the tempo, the dynamics and the spirit of each hymn, as well as defining the phrases throughout. He leads either in response to the conductor or, if no conductor is present, at his own discretion. The former is leadership under subordination; the latter is direct leadership.

b. In accompaniment. Etherington states that "too many organists are much better prepared for their voluntaries and postludes than for their duties as accompanists."[3] In addition to the artistic ability required to perform, accompanying requires sensitivity to the desires of others. The organist is in a supporting role, in which the ideas projected must not be his own, but must be in accord with those of the performer or director with whom he is working. In preparing to accompany, the organist should consider the following:

(1) The musical and textual demands of the composition. A thorough study of the tempo, dynamics and expression markings, plus a review of the words, considering their high points and natural phrase separations are basic preparations which should be made before rehearsing with the performer. In the preparation for accompanying hymns, gospel songs, or other compositions which do not indicate expression and dynamics, it is important to study every stanza of the text for contrasts and unusual phrasings.

(2) The nature and position of the accompaniment. All accompaniments do not serve in the same manner. In most music, the accompaniment takes on one of three different personalities, that of background to the performer, of complement to the spirit of the

---

[3]C. L. Etherington, *The Organist and Choirmaster* (New York: Macmillan Co., 1952), p. 5.

performance, or of complete independence. At times these positions are obvious, but frequently the entire musical work must be carefully analyzed to determine them. The following are suggested approaches to be made to each.

(a) An unpretentious background. There are times when the accompaniment should be hardly noticeable. This is especially true on a quiet, reflective plainsong, spiritual, hymn of devotion, prayer response, or when accompanying a work which is normally *a cappella*. Only the basic stops (usually 8-foot soft diapasons and flutes) should be used, and all vocal phrases should be observed. Such accompaniments are usually easy to read, but demand a great deal of sensitivity to perform.

(b) A complementary accompaniment. More frequently the accompaniment will take on the dynamic characteristics of the performance parts, but will contribute bridges and interludes between the vocal phrases, and complement the singers with countermelodies and other accompanimental patterns. This is the type most frequently employed in anthems and sacred solos, and the most desirable type of improvisation on the renditions of hymns and gospel songs.

(c) An independent idea. The sacred art song, oratorio excerpt, extended chorale prelude and other types of anthems and solos often employ accompaniments which take on characters independent to the styles and moods expressed in the performers' parts. In this type there exists a coworking relationship between accompanist and performers. Examples of this would be Bach's "Jesu, Joy of Man's Desiring" or a picturesque recitative ·such as "And God Made the Firmament" from *The Creation* by Haydn, in which the accompaniment is depicting the clouds, the fire, the thunders and the showers, alternately between the recitative passages. The difficulty in performing is caused by the inability of either accompanist or singers to depend upon each other for tempo, mood and dynamics.

(3) The desires of the performer. Most performers exercise the right to make their own interpretation of the music and even to adjust phrases and markings to suit their own individual tastes and abilities. The accompanist must be sensitive to these adjustments and should mark them during rehearsal, yet at the same time should be prepared for any changes which may occur during the performance. If the text and the music have been well examined it is easier to anticipate where the changes may occur.

(4) The general characteristics of the performer. It is most

helpful to know the performer and his limitations, vocal range, size of voice, degree of musicianship and general style of singing. A knowledge of these characteristics will aid the organist in selecting stop registrations, in preparing for necessary transpositions and in anticipating what changes may occur during the performance.

(5) The performer's attitude toward the accompaniment. Both singers and directors have varied concepts of what place of prominence the accompaniment should have. Some depend upon it for leadership; some desire great support from it; while others prefer it to be strictly in subjection to their desires. A knowledge of these attitudes is most important to the accompanist, as it determines to what extent he must lead and to what degree he is subordinate.

c. In service playing. The organist is responsible for the establishing of continuity within the church service. This does not suggest that he should play continually during the service, but rather that he should provide the necessary bridges to prevent any lulls during the service, as well as to establish the climate which will complement the worship. He should consult the pastor as to when these bridges are desired. If the pastor agrees on their importance, the following factors should be observed:

(1) Balance. Even as there are times when background music is essential to diffuse any undesirable sounds (of people standing or sitting) and prevent any dead spots, there are also times when silence itself lends to the spirit and atmosphere of the moment. Just as in a symphony, the worship service must have a balance of musical bridges and moments of silence.

(2) Aspects of worship. Every well-balanced service consists of a variety of worship attitudes which include praise, prayer, challenge and meditation. The organ interludes should serve as bridges from one phase to another, and should be so constructed that the change of spirit is felt. As a rule, however, the organist should never play during the reading of the Scripture lesson or the pastoral prayer, as this may become a detracting element to these important parts of worship. Background music is sometimes used effectively under short invocations, benedictions or calls to worship, but becomes tedious when continuing for any great length of time.

d. In solo performance. While the prelude, offertory and postlude are usually referred to as service music, they are distinctive in that they involve solo literature. The church organist should have very little difficulty finding appropriate solo material for these parts of the service. There are collections of music on the market today, ranging from the very simple to the most challenging organ pieces.

In addition to these, many hymns and anthems can be used easily and effectively by carefully selecting the stop registrations for interest and expressiveness.

The greatest function of the organ solo is to contribute to the act and attitude of worship. Whereas the organist's solos usually come at a time when worshipers are being seated, offering plates are being passed or people are leaving the sanctuary, he should not function as a mere time filler, but should be performing the following ministries:

(1) Preparing minds and hearts. The organ is often referred to as a means of "creating an atmosphere"; however, its ministry of creating atmosphere is designed to establish attitudes of worship in the minds of those who do not know how to worship, and in the hearts of those who do.

(2) Permitting worship. After attitudes have been established, the organist must be sure that his music not only "leads" but also "lets." The worshiper must be permitted to worship in the manner which will best meet his spiritual need of the hour. Often a familiar hymn tune will detract from his spirit of inner worship, or a mood expressed in the music will prevent him from expressing his own feelings to God. As a general rule, the prelude should be neutral music of a quiet, meditative nature; the offertory can be more subjective, providing the subject lends itself to the nature of worship expressed in the service; and the postlude should be of a challenging and encouraging spirit.

(3) Presenting the subject of worship. According to Lorenz, "In his prelude, he [the organist] becomes the temporary chairman whose duty it is to announce the purpose of the meeting."[4] Usually the purpose which he "announces" should be that of worship itself, but on certain occasions it is appropriate to introduce a subjective thought. This is true of special occasions, such as Easter, Thanksgiving and Christmas, or when the church activities are all centered around a specific theme, such as evangelism, missions, church anniversary or communion. These subjects can be introduced through settings of familiar hymns commonly associated with the themes, or through standard organ selections portraying the mood elements which will be associated with the subject, such as triumph on Easter Sunday and introspection on Worldwide Communion Sunday.

2. General influences of the organist

---

[4] E. S. Lorenz, *The Singing Church* (Nashville: Cokesbury Press, 1938), p. 28.

"The organist speaks through the organ."[5] His ministry is more than a contribution to the service, it is an influence of worship. He proves his dedication by his dependability and his obvious preparation for the task. He displays his musicianship through the type of performances he gives and the quality of music he uses. He reveals his knowledge of the teachings of the Bible through his interpretation of the music. He shows his understanding of the beliefs and practices of the church by the way he handles the service, the sacraments and the special practices carried on in the worship. His life carries a great influence wherever he goes, especially as he fellowships among the people of the church, displaying not only his love for the people but also his love for God. As Havergal so aptly put it, "Besides fingers and feet, a soul."

3. *Qualifications of the organist*

a. Sight-reading ability. Although it is good practice to prepare all music in advance of the rehearsals and performances, this cannot always be followed. Sight-reading ability is essential, not only for emergency purposes but also for speeding up the process of learning all music. This ability can be easily obtained through a consistent observance of the structure of music and slow, rhythmic practice; however, it often takes years of practice to develop efficiency in the skill.

b. Ability to adapt piano music to the organ. The organist is often faced with the responsibility of playing piano music on the organ. Some pianistic devices, such as arpeggios, repeated chords, octave scales, large skips and others which depend largely on the sustaining pedal for effectiveness, must be revised to suit the organ. This is usually accomplished by converting all arpeggios and patterns so that they will fit into one hand position, and sustaining most of the chords or repeating only one of the notes in the chord to establish the rhythmic pattern.

c. Improvisation. The organist also faces the problem of providing interesting accompaniments or solos based on the hymn or gospel song which is notated for voices alone. The general principles to follow are: sustain chords rather than repeating them; carry most phrases through rather than separating them when the performer takes a breath; enhance the beauty of the piece by occasionally playing alto or tenor segments on a solo stop or employing passing notes, tasteful reharmonizations and accompanimental patterns.

d. Transposition. One of the most difficult techniques to develop

[5] J. N. Ashton, *Music in Worship* (Boston: Pilgrim Press, 1943), p. 215.

is that of transposition, but it is frequently requested and greatly advantageous to performers with limited or unusual vocal ranges. A certain amount of this may be obtained by ear, but this method is not dependable. In order to transpose correctly and confidently, the organist must be able to analyze the melodic and harmonic structure of the piece. Harmonic analysis enables him to see each chord as it relates to a key, therefore enabling him to play the same progression of chords in any key desired. This, however, takes years of training and practice, but its accomplishment is well worth the time and effort necessary for its obtainment.

4. *Practical problems confronting the organist*

a. The performer's need to adapt to church music. An organist who is highly skilled in performance must make certain adaptations to meet the needs of the church position. There is sufficient service material available, including standard organ works, anthems and oratorio selections, which require the best of ability. If he is judicious in choosing his music, the skilled organist will be able to put to good use the technical facility he has obtained. However, he must refrain from using pieces demanding excess technical display if they do not contribute to his ministry in worship.

b. The pianist's inability to adjust to organ techniques. Many church organists have been trained in piano, with little or no background in organ. While his reading ability and finger facility may be adequate, a pianist must develop the skills of legato playing, pedal technique and coordination of feet and hands. He must also learn to understand stop combinations and command at least a limited amount of organ repertoire.

c. The temptation of excessive expression. The organ is a colorful instrument. Its tone colors can contribute to the developing of an attitude and spirit of worship, but must not be used in excess. Two of the most common faults in expression are the overuse of the pedal, which results in a constant fluctuation of volume, and the overemphasis of theatrical effects which create what might be considered an ethereal mood but not a worshipful attitude.

d. The lack of understanding of acoustics. The sound which the organ produces is influenced by brick and mortar as well as by pipes and blowers. Many organists fail to consider this when preparing stop combinations, performing and accompanying. A thorough understanding of the church acoustical characteristics will aid him in getting the best sound from the instrument and in developing the best possible ensemble with the choir, soloists and organ.

Church Pianist

Despite the fact that the organ is generally considered the church instrument, pianos are still in constant use in church work. In some churches, it is the only instrument available. It is used in almost every church for rehearsals, in Sunday school and youth departments, and is a complementing instrument to the organ in some services.

1. Functions of the church pianist

Except for the stop registrations and basic repertoire, the principles applied to the organist, his functions in leadership, accompaniment, service playing and solo performances, will all apply to the pianist when in a similar position of responsibility.

2. Requirements of the church pianist

a. General technical ability. The technical facility necessary for playing church literature is just as demanding as any other kind, but because of the chordal structure of church music, particularly hymns, the most critical areas are legato pedaling, chord playing, tonal balance, and phrasing techniques.

b. Accompaniment for children's voices. The beauty of sound in a child's voice is greatly dependent upon a sensitive, rhythmic and flowing accompaniment. The pianist must:

(1) Provide support without playing heavily, so that the child will respond confidently but not forcefully.

(2) Make the phrases very obvious, to help the child be at ease in his singing, as well as to better express the real content of the text.

(3) Play a colorful, flowing and rather independent accompaniment (that will help the child feel rhythmic pulses) and sense the "mood idea" of the piece.

(4) If necessary, transpose (discussed under "The Organist") the music to keys suitable to undeveloped or changing voices.

c. Hymn playing ability. Hymn playing is one of the most difficult tasks confronting the pianist. It is almost impossible for him to give adequate support to a congregation when playing the hymn as written. Because of the percussive nature of the piano tone, plus the fact that it cannot be sustained for a very long duration, it is necessary to expand the four notes indicated in the hymnal to larger chords which will be repeated in various positions when the hymnal calls for a sustained tone. The following steps are necessary in developing a good command of hymn playing techniques:

(1) Learn to think by chords. This will enable the pianist to think of the four voices for improvisation. The chord can be played

in several sizes, inversions and positions on the piano, and can be constructed in patterns and arpeggios.

(2) Develop several basic chord styles. The pianist should have command of several contrasting congregational styles so that his playing will be able to reflect the spirit of the devotional as well as the majestic hymn, and so that there may be different approaches to the stanzas of each hymn.

(3) Study the characteristics of hymns in comparison to standard piano literature and accompaniments to vocal solos. This will help the pianist expand his resources of styles, especially for accompanying.

(4) Practice technical devices which can be used in hymn playing, such as scales, chords and chord patterns, arpeggios and octaves. All of these take months of consistent practice before they can be played well.

3. Repertoire for the church pianist

The pianist does not have the reserve of service material that is available for the church organist. In fact, very little piano music has been written that is both pianistic in style and adaptable to service usage. The following sources should be explored to find music which is suitable for preludes, offertories, postludes, and other solo responsibilities:

a. Selected pieces by Bach, Handel and other composers of that period

b. Slow movements from the classic sonatas by Beethoven, Mozart and Haydn

c. Organ chorale preludes which have been adapted for piano

d. Organ works which do not require pedal

e. Selected pieces by Brahms and Franck which are not too florid in style

f. Tastefully written hymn settings for piano

The Vocal Soloist

The vocal soloists in some churches are employed in the same manner as the choir directors and organists. Other churches use one or more of their choir members as soloists in a voluntary capacity. Aside from salary stipulations, there should be no difference in the functions, responsibilities and qualifications of the paid soloist and the volunteer.

He may function in one of the following ways:

(1) As a part of a solo quartet, to sing solos, and in duet and quartet combinations.

(2) Same as above, with the additional responsibility of assisting in the choir as sectional leader.

(3) As a regular member of the choir, with occasional opportunities for solo work.

1. Background of solo singing

Solo singing has been practiced throughout the history of the Christian church and even, to some extent, in Old Testament times. It is believed that the song of victory in Exodus 15 was sung by Moses alone, and responded to antiphonally by the children of Israel; and it is even more evident that the response in verse 21 was by Miriam, accompanied by all the women "with timbrels and with dances" (v. 20). This suggests the possible method used before the temple worship was established.

When the music training program was developed in the time of David, the music responsibilities were placed in the hands of the Levitical choirs and instrumentalists, and soloists were not used to any extent, if at all.

Solo singing became firmly established in worship in the early Christian church, when the cantor sang portions of the Psalms alone, with antiphonal response from the choir. As instruments became gradually accepted back into the church, the solo voice was given more prominence. This is evidenced by the wealth of solo motets with instrumental accompaniments which were written for church use in the fourteenth century, and the many solos which were included in the motets and cantatas of the Baroque period.

2. The ministry of the soloist

There are contradictory opinions concerning the use of solos in the church. Some forbid its practice on the basis that it does not lend itself to corporate worship. According to Halter, the argument usually is that "it is an intrusion upon this community of worship for a 'star' singer to arise and, by singing a solo, introduce a personal and theatrical element."[6]

Halter defends its use, however, by stating, "It is perfectly possible for a solo to be used and presented in such a manner as to aid rather than hinder the worship of all present."[7] This has been evidenced in biblical history and in the early Christian church as well as in the history of revivals. This was seen in the ministries of Ira D. Sankey during the Moody revivals. Homer Rodeheaver, in connection with the Billy Sunday campaigns of the early twenti-

---

[6] Carl Halter, *The Practice of Sacred Music* (St. Louis: Concordia Publishing House, 1955), p. 18.

[7] *Loc. cit.*

eth century, and George Beverly Shea, in the Billy Graham crusades of this generation, have had similar ministries. To fully appreciate the extent of the ministry of the soloist, it is important to consider three ways in which his solo can function in worship.

a. It presents a message to the individual. Although the worship service is designed for corporate participation, it still must minister to the individual. The soloist possesses this power of ministering to the individual, and of speaking to him "man to man." The highest use of a human voice is to reach a human heart. Sellers says, "Some of the most effective and lasting messages given to the world have been rendered by the sacred soloists."[8]

Many of the truths contained in music today are personal messages to the individual based on doctrines or admonitions from the Bible, such as "He that dwelleth in the secret place . . ." (Ps. 91), "Seek ye the Lord, while he may be found" (Isa. 55:6), "God so loved the world that . . . whosoever believeth . . ." (John 3:16), "Let your light so shine before men . . ." (Matt. 5:16). Others are based on texts of human composition, such as "How Sweet the Name of Jesus Sounds in a Believer's Ear" (Newton) and "Take Time to Be Holy" (Longstaff).

b. The solo represents the individual. Whereas the choir represents the entire congregation, the soloist personifies the man in the pew. This is done in the following ways:

(1) In communion with God. The soloist represents man's personal prayer of penitence, dedication or supplication, by using music based on Scripture passages, such as "I Will Extol Thee, O Lord" (Ps. 30) and "Create in Me a Clean Heart" (Ps. 51), or on texts such as "O Master, Let Me Walk with Thee" (Gladden), "Jesus, Keep Me Near the Cross" (Crosby) and "Jesus, I Come" (Sleeper).

(2) In testimony of his personal experience or desire. The soloist also puts into music the expression of the testimony or need of the individual, again using Scripture passages, such as "I Waited for the Lord" (Ps. 40), "I Sought the Lord, and He Heard Me" (Ps. 34:4), "I Know in Whom I Have Believed" (II Tim. 1:12). Or the many songs of personal testimony and challenge may be used, such as "Am I a Soldier of the Cross?" (Watts), "All Things in Jesus I Find" (Loes) and "O for a Closer Walk with God" (Cowper).

c. The solo portrays the messenger. In opera, in oratorios, and

---

[8] E. O. Sellers, *Worship, Why and How* (Grand Rapids: Zondervan Publishing House, 1941), p. 18.

in some cantatas, the soloist usually portrays the life of another person. The solo literature of the church consists not only in selections from oratorios and cantatas which are so designed but also in other selections which either quote or are based on the words of biblical messengers, including Christ himself, the greatest Messenger of truth.

Some texts which contain the words of biblical persons are: "My Soul Doth Magnify the Lord" (Luke 1:46-49), the words of Mary; "The Voice of One Crying in the Wilderness" (John 1:23), the words of John the Baptist; "I Know in Whom I Have Believed" (previously mentioned), the words of Paul. Texts which portray Christ and use his own words are plentiful. A few suggestions are: "Come unto Me, All Ye That Labor" (Matt. 11:28-30), "I Am the Light of the World" (John 8:12), and "O Jerusalem, Which Killest the Prophets" (Luke 13:34).

One of the most significant compliments that can be given a singer is that he so capably portrayed the person of whom he sang, that the listener was able to "see" this person through the singer. Just as it is possible for the bass soloist to relive the part of Elijah in Mendelssohn's great work, it is possible that Christ can be seen through the dedicated singer who portrays Him in song.

3. The responsibilities of the soloist

The soloist's responsibilities lie in both musical presentation and attitude of life, as indicated in the imperatives for all church musicians. In relation to his particular ministries, he must:

a. Understand the message which he presents and experience its results, particularly in relation to redemption.

b. Be a worthy representative of the congregation in his daily conduct and Christian testimony.

c. Know Christ intimately enough that the Holy Spirit can work through him in exemplifying and portraying the life of Christ.

4. The choice of material

The guiding motive should be to express, not to impress. The text, to be rightly expressed, must be wedded to music of the same spirit and sung in like manner. In short, a simple style for a simple thought, a majestic style for a majestic thought, and an exuberant style for an exuberant thought.

The music should be not only an acceptable vehicle but the best that one can find to present, represent or portray the message therein.

The following are a few of the vocal forms which can be used by the church soloist:

a. Solo motet and cantata. Mention has already been made of the fourteenth century solo motets. Solo cantatas were written during the seventeenth century by Buxtehude and other composers of that day. Although these resembled the motets, they were structured more like the choral cantatas of that period. Later in the classic era, Joseph Haydn also wrote several solo cantatas.

b. Song cycles. Song cycles are sets of songs based on poems written by one author. Some of the sacred song cycles are based on Scripture, such as the Dvorak "Biblical Songs" and the "Musical Settings of Sacred Psalms" by Ward-Stephens. Others are written to sacred poetry, such as "Musical Settings of Sacred Words," also by Ward-Stephens.

c. Sacred art songs. This is an all-inclusive classification of sacred solos of a larger form than the chorale, hymn and gospel song, but not in any of the above styles or taken from any choral works. The nineteenth and twentieth centuries have produced many composers of such solos which are practical for church use. Among many others, they include John Prindle Scott, James MacDermid, Carl Mueller, Roberta Bitgood, Eric Thiman, Randall Thompson and Leo Sowerby.

d. Other sources. The vocal soloist has many other sources from which he may gather repertoire, including the larger form choral cantatas and oratorios, most of which contain arias and solos suitable for independent use. With much discretion and care, he may also adapt certain anthems, chorales and hymns for solo usage. And, for a means of expressing his personal testimony and Christian experiences, he may wish to use the gospel song.

5. *The problems encountered*

Some of the problems which usually confront the soloist in choosing music are:

a. Correct keys and ranges. No solo should demand the highest or lowest notes in the singer's voice. It should lie for the most part in his more comfortable range, with occasional high and low points at least two steps within his limitations.

b. Suitable dynamics and styles. The strength and control of the voice, the ability to sing expressively, dramatically, with warmth, or with emotion—all these are necessary considerations in selecting solos.

c. Balance of repertoire. One of the temptations of a singer is to overuse a certain style or idiom. This is sometimes caused by an awareness of his limitations, but more frequently by personal preference. Two ways to combat this are:

(1) By choosing a balance of texts to include three aspects of the singer's ministry (to present, represent, portray).

(2) By using a balance of forms including larger works (oratorio selections and sacred solos), hymns of devotion or meditation and gospel songs of testimony and experience.

6. *The technique needed*

"There is no opposition between spirituality and technique; as a matter of fact, the spiritual singer ought to have the finest vocal training and musicianship."[9] Technique is synonymous with method. It is the source of improved methods for use in spiritual singing. The church soloist needs a composite of that which is endowed by the Holy Spirit (I John 2:27) and that which has been achieved by training. There are serious complications in combining these two elements which at first appear to be contrary to one another. The singer who would sing "in the Spirit" seems to have no time to think about technique, while the technically conscious student almost forgets the content of his message because of all that he must consider in correct execution. This often becomes a source of discouragement to the student who has entered into vocal study with the sole purpose of making his ministry more effective.

The problem is not incompatibility but concentration. The following procedure may be helpful in attaining a combination of the two:

a. Concentrate on techniques. The vocal student's career must begin with an unreserved dedication to the study of techniques. He should practice correct breathing methods, tone production, phrasing and diction until they are sufficiently in his control.

b. Concentrate on texts. Separate from the student's vocal study, he should examine sacred texts, prayerfully seeking to discover and understand all the truths they contain, how he can best express their meaning to others, and how the words relate to the music. Memorization will no doubt be a natural result of this study, as well as association of melody with rhythm.

c. Apply techniques to music. When the vocal student first begins to sing the music, his prime concern should be correct singing principles. Although he will employ the words, concentrating on the vowels, consonants and phrases, he may be unable to give much thought to their spiritual importance until he has succeeded in conquering these technical problems.

d. "Sing with the spirit and with the understanding." After the

[9] G. Urang, *Church Music—For the Glory of God* (Moline, Ill.: Christian Service Foundation, 1956), pp. 210, 211.

music has been mastered, the principles of good singing will serve as a natural vehicle to the spiritual truth found in the text. The separation of time of concentration on technique and on text will have permitted the singer to learn the principles before having to apply them.

RECOMMENDED READING

For the Music Director:

GARRETTSON, R. L. *Conducting Choral Music*. Boston: Allyn and Bacon, Inc., 1961.

GEHRKENS, K. W. *Essentials in Conducting*. Philadelphia: Oliver Ditson Company, 1919.

HJORTSVANG, CARL. *The Amateur Choir Director*. Nashville: Abingdon Press, 1941.

NININGER, RUTH. *Growing a Musical Church*. Nashville: Broadman Press, 1947.

For the Organist:

ASHTON, J. N. *Music in Worship*. Boston: Pilgrim Press, 1943.

BACON, A. *The True Function of Church Music*. Stockton: Printwell Press, 1953.

LOVELACE, A. C. *The Organist and Hymn Playing*. Nashville: Abingdon Press, 1962.

For the Pianist:

MATHIS, W. S. *The Pianist and Church Music*. Nashville: Abingdon Press, 1962.

MOORE, G. *The Unashamed Accompanist*. New York: Macmillan Co., 1946.

RUBINSTEIN, B. *The Pianist's Approach to Sight-Reading and Memorizing*. New York: Carl Fischer, Inc., 1950.

For the Vocal Soloist:

HALTER, C. *The Practice of Sacred Music*. St. Louis: Concordia Publishing House, 1956.

LOVELACE, A. C., and RICE, W. C. *Music and Worship in the Church*. Nashville: Abingdon Press, 1960.

MARSHALL, M. *The Singer's Manual of English Diction*. New York: G. Schirmer, Inc., 1953.

RICE, W. C. *Basic Principles of Singing*. Nashville: Abingdon Press, 1961.

URANG, G. *Church Music—For the Glory of God*. Moline, Ill.: Christian Service Foundation, 1956.

Chapter 8

HYMNODY

Introduction

Aside from the performer himself, there is nothing that influences the effectiveness of a ministry in music more than the literature which is used. Church music literature is the connecting link between the messenger and the recipient. Its weaknesses lessen the means of communication; its strong points add impact to the message which it bears. For this reason it is of extreme importance that the literature one uses is fully understood and carefully selected to fulfill the function for which it is intended.

Church music literature comprises two areas: hymnody and service music. Hymnody is that music which is commonly associated with the layman, while service music is that which is performed by the church musician and therefore is not bound by the limitations of the congregation. There are many points of natural overlapping of the two types. Occasionally a congregation will join in the singing of the service music, particularly in some liturgical churches. More frequently the hymn will find its way into the repertoire of the musician, serving as a basis for an anthem, organ prelude or instrumental setting.

The Hymn

The hymn is the center of church music. It is the most commonly used and understood form of music. The study of hymnology is an inexhaustible one which demands much time and effort to comprehend fully, yet it is possible to gain a fair understanding of it through a synoptic approach such as is given here, in which the three general periods of its development are observed, along with the many forms which make up hymnody today. The three general periods are: the early Christian era, the early Protestant movements, and the modern period.

DEVELOPMENT OF HYMNODY IN THE CHRISTIAN CHURCH

Early Christian Era

Biblical Settings
Old Testament authors:
   David and other
      psalmists
   Moses
   Solomon
   Isaiah
New Testament authors:
   Paul, John and others

Greek Hymnody
Clement of Alexandria
   (150-c.220)
Synesius of Cyrene
   (375-c.430)
Stephen of Mar Saba
   (725-794)
Andrew of Crete
   (660-732)
John of Damascus
   (c.700-c.754)

Latin Hymnody
Musical Trends:
   Ambrose of Milan
      (340-397)
   Pope Gregory
      (590-604)
Authors:
   Theodulph of Orleans
      (760-821)
   Bernard of Clairvaux
      (1091-1153)
   Bernard of Cluny
      (12th century)
   Francis of Assisi
      (1182-1226)

Early Protestant Movements

German Chorale
Authors:
   Martin Luther
      (1483-1546)
   Philipp Nicolai
      (1556-1608)
   Martin Rinkart
      (1586-1649)
   Georg Neumark
      (1621-1681)
   Paul Gerhardt
      (1607-1676)
   Count Zinzendorf
      (1700-1760)
Composers:
   Hans Hassler
      (1564-1612)
      (1598-1662)
   Johann Crüger
   Johann S. Bach
      (1685-1750)

Metrical Psalmbooks
Genevan Psalter (1562)
Sternhold and Hopkins'
   Book of Psalms (1562)
Scottish Psalter (1564)
Bay Psalm Book (1640)

English Hymnody
Isaac Watts (1674-1748)
Charles Wesley
   (1707-1788)
Thomas Ken
   (1637-1711)
Philip Doddridge
   (1702-1751)
John Newton
   (1725-1807)
William Cowper
   (1731-1800)

Reginald Heber
   (1783-1826)
Charlotte Elliott
   (1789-1871)
Frances R. Havergal
   (1836-1879)
American Hymnody
Composer:
   Lowell Mason
      (1792-1872)
   "Father of American
      Hymnody"
Authors:
   Timothy Dwight
      (1752-1817)
   Thomas Hastings
      (1784-1872)
   George W. Doane
      (1799-1859)
   Phillips Brooks
      (1835-1893)
   Mary A. Lathbury
      (1841-1913)
   Ray Palmer
      (1808-1887)

Modern Period

Revival of Early Music
Translator from Greek:
   Henry M. Dexter
      (1821-1890)
Translators from Latin:
   Edward Caswall
      (1814-1878)
   John M. Neale
      (1818-1866)
   Catherine Winkworth
      (1829-1878)

Gospel Song
Early writers:
   Philip P. Bliss
      (1838-1876)
   Robert Lowry
      (1826-1899)
   Ira D. Sankey
      (1840-1908)
   James McGranahan
      (1840-1907)
   Fanny J. Crosby
      (1820-1915)

Later Gospel Song Trends
The chorus:
   Charles H. Alexander
   Wendell Loveless
   Harry Dixon Loes
   Sidney Cox
Gospel song special:
   Norman J. Clayton
   C. F. Weigle
   Phil Kerr
   John Peterson
   Merrill Dunlop

William H. Doane
(1832-1915)
Charles H. Gabriel
(1856-1932)
Recent writers:
Homer Rodeheaver
Haldor Lillenas
A. H. Ackley
B. D. Ackley

Early Christian Era

1. The Psalms

The use of the psalms was carried over from the Old Testament times to the time of Christ, who no doubt sang them in the temple and the synagogues as a youth. They are known to have been used at the various festivities in which Jesus participated during his ministry, including the Passover (John 2:13) and the annual Feast of Tabernacles (John 7:14).

The early church is believed to have carried out the tradition of singing psalms antiphonally between the priest and the congregation or choir, with instrumental interludes occurring at the points marked "selah." This marking generally comes at a dividing place between two contrasting thoughts, such as a call to praise followed by a testimony of God's goodness, as found in Psalms 24, 47 and 81; or between the words of the Psalmist and the words of God himself, as found in Psalm 50.

2. Other Old Testament texts

Texts from other books of the Old Testament were also used, including portions of the songs of Solomon, the songs of Moses (Exodus 15:1-19; Deut. 32:1-43), that of Miriam (Exodus 15:21), and several verses in Isaiah, such as

> Holy, holy, holy, is the Lord of hosts,
> The whole earth is full of thy glory.
>
> ISAIAH 6:3

3. New Testament songs

Early Christians were encouraged by Paul to sing "psalms and hymns and spiritual songs" (Col. 3:16). Some think the spiritual songs referred to several New Testament texts which contained doctrine and personal expressions of man. Some of those believed to have been used are:

Ephesians 5:14—a cry for spiritual awakening
I Timothy 3:16—the doctrine of the Trinity
II Timothy 2:11—life after death
Revelation 4:11—God the Creator

4. Greek hymnody

Hymns written by man were known to be in existence as early as the second century. The oldest known hymn is attributed to Clement of Alexandria in about A.D. 170.

> Shepherd of tender youth,
> Guiding in loving truth,
>   Through devious ways;
> Christ, our triumphant King,
> We come Thy Name to sing,
> Hither the children bring
>   Tributes of praise.
>
> Translated by Henry Martin Dexter,
> 19th century

5. Latin hymnody

One of the most significant eras of hymnody, both musically and textually, was the period between the third and seventh centuries. Under the leadership of Bishop Ambrose of Milan (340-397), old tunes were revised and set to uniform rhythmic patterns which corresponded with the rhythm of speech. Many of the original Ambrosian chants are still used in the Roman Catholic liturgy.

In the seventh century, Pope Gregory revised other melodies, making them even more expressive. He also created new scale systems which opened avenues to future composers. One of our present tunes, now known as Hamburg, originated from the Gregorian period. This is the melody which has been arranged by Lowell Mason and is commonly associated with Isaac Watts' text, "When I Survey the Wondrous Cross."

The plainsong, a title later ascribed to the chants of Ambrose and Gregory, is still much in use today. One familiar example is "O Come, O Come, Emmanuel" (attributed to the 13th century, arranged by Thomas Helmore in 1854).

A few of the translations from early Latin texts include:

"All Glory, Laud, and Honor"—Theodulph of Orleans (760-821)

"Jesus, the Very Thought of Thee"—Bernard of Clairvaux (12th century)

"Jerusalem the Golden"—Bernard of Cluny (12th century)

"All Creatures of Our God and King"—Francis of Assisi (1182-1226)

Early Protestant Movements

1. The German chorale

The Protestant Reformation in Germany under Martin Luther became a dynamic force behind several new trends in church music. Luther himself was a musician and is believed to have written some original hymn tunes and texts. However, he is better known as a translator, arranger and compiler. It was through Luther's influence that the chorale was born. The chorale is a hymn of doctrine, based on scriptural truths penned by early Latin writers or contemporaries of Luther, and set to a familiar German folk melody. Since Luther's time, many of the greatest contributions to hymnody have been written in German chorale style. One good example is Luther's own "A Mighty Fortress Is Our God." The familiar Lenten hymn, "O Sacred Head, Now Wounded," is also a product of the German school, having been based on a text of the twelfth century which was translated into German by Paul Gerhardt shortly before the time of Bach, and set to a melody by Hans Hassler, with the harmonization supplied by Bach.

2. The Psalter and the English hymn

Possibly our two most common forms of hymnody today are the Psalm setting and the English hymn. Their backgrounds stem from the unrest and dissatisfaction in the English churches over Roman domination in the sixteenth century. When the Pope excommunicated Henry VIII, many of the people followed him to set up their own forms of worship, which would exclude all Latin forms and hymns. During the reign of Henry and his successor, Edward VI, little or no music was used, since there was nothing to replace the Latin hymns. However, Protestantism continued to prosper until the death of Edward, when his half sister, Bloody Mary, took over the throne, at which time all Roman rituals were brought back into the church. Almost three hundred Christians were then martyred for refusing to return to Roman ways of worship, while others fled to Switzerland and elsewhere on the Continent.

a. The Psalter. Those who fled to Switzerland became influenced by John Calvin, and through him were introduced to the singing of metrical psalms. When they returned to England at the death of Queen Mary, they brought with them these psalters. The psalter is a compilation of psalms set to a strict meter by rewording certain phrases. One familiar example is the setting of the Twenty-third Psalm as sung to the Crimond tune.

> The Lord's my Shepherd, I'll not want;
>   He makes me down to lie
> In pastures green; He leadeth me
>   The quiet waters by.
>   *Scottish Psalter,* 1650

English poets soon began to set the psalms to meter, and composers such as Christopher Tye, Thomas Tallis and John Taverner began writing tunes to fit these words. Thus, English hymnody was born. Books of original psalters were soon printed, the oldest known collections being the *Book of Psalms* by Sternhold and Hopkins in 1562, and the *Scottish Psalter* in 1564.

The singing of psalters was eventually brought to America and, in 1640, the *Bay Psalm Book* was published. Significantly, this was the first book to be printed in America.

b. The hymn. An outgrowth of the psalter was the hymn. Although the word is used broadly as including all forms of church songs, the hymn form is specifically a text based on Scripture or doctrine, but written in man's own words. It differs from the German chorale in that it is a freer interpretation of the Scriptures. It differs from the psalter in that it is not confined to the Psalms, nor is it necessarily restricted to any one passage of Scripture.

Two of the most influential figures in English hymnody are: *Isaac Watts* (1674–1748), known as the "Father of English Hymnody." As a boy, Isaac was disturbed by the poor-quality texts being sung in the church. Usually, each Sunday the cantor would haphazardly devise verses to be sung to one of the few familiar tunes. Often they were nothing less than sacrilegious. On a particular Sunday the cantor brought forth these words:

> Ye monsters of the bubbling deep,
> Your Maker's praise spout out;
> Up from the sands, ye coddlings, peep
> And wag your tails about.

When young Isaac openly criticized these words, his father challenged him to try to write better ones, a challenge he readily accepted. When the elder Watts showed the words to the cantor, Isaac was commissioned to write words for every Sunday service. This he did for the following two years, bringing into being many of our best loved texts, including "Alas, and Did My Saviour Bleed?" "O God, Our Help in Ages Past," "Joy to the World" and "When I Survey the Wondrous Cross."

Charles Wesley (1707–1788), one of the founders of Methodism, who wrote approximately 6,500 hymns, undoubtedly more than any other person. His hymns were designed as expressions of personal faith and Christian responsibilities, as clearly revealed in the many hymns which are still being used today, such as "A Charge to Keep I Have," "Jesus, Lover of My Soul" and "Hark! the Herald Angels Sing."

American hymnody

One of the first composers of American hymns was Lowell Mason (1792-1872), who composed and arranged many tunes, such as "When I Survey the Wondrous Cross" (Hamburg), "Work, for the Night Is Coming" (Work Song) and "My Faith Looks Up to Thee" (Olivet).

Although he did not write words, Mason is known as the "Father of American Hymnody." Texts were written by many American authors during the eighteenth and nineteenth centuries, some of whom are listed on the chart accompanying this chapter.

Modern Period

In the nineteenth and twentieth centuries, hymnody began to move in two opposite directions, one to uncover the old styles and the other to develop new styles. It was during this time that the old Latin and Greek hymns were translated into English and restored to use, and also the gospel song was born.

1. Revival of the plainsong

It was around 1860 when translators such as Catherine Winkworth, John M. Neale and others began to translate the previously discarded Latin and Greek hymns. By that time, many of the original prejudices were forgotten and Protestants were then searching for new tools to use to worship God. Through these translators, a rich heritage of music literature was reactivated after lying dormant for more than three hundred years.

2. The gospel song

At the same time, a new and almost revolutionary trend was taking place in evangelism. Sensing the need for songs that would give a more personal impact to the message of the gospel, Evangelist D. L. Moody and his musical associate, Ira D. Sankey, began using gospel songs in their worldwide meetings. The songs were used, not as a substitute for the standard hymns of doctrine and faith, but rather to personify the message found in these hymns. Although this was the first extended usage of gospel songs, composers such as Robert Lowry and Philip P. Bliss had been writing them for about a quarter of a century. Sankey contributed to the literature by writing "The Ninety and Nine," "Grace, 'Tis a Charming Sound" and many others, but his greatest service to the propagation of the new style was his compilation of the Moody-Sankey songbooks, which made gospel songs available to the people.

The unique characteristic of the gospel song text is its emphasis on personal testimony, which distinguishes it from the hymn of worship and meditation. For this reason, it fulfills an important function in providing a balance in church hymnody. It was also created for the purposes of reaching the emotions and provoking a definite decision in the heart. Its words are usually direct and unadorned, and its music is melodious and singable. It often concludes with a short refrain which summarizes the message of the stanzas.

The gospel song movement has also led to two other kinds of gospel music:

a. The chorus, a shorter form of the gospel song, containing a simple and direct truth which is repeated frequently in its one stanza. Its greatest merit is its simplicity of thought, making it readily understood by children and easy to remember. Choruses originated in the early twentieth century, when Charles H. Alexander and others began using them in evangelistic campaigns. The earliest known publication of choruses is the *Alexander Gospel Songs* (1909), which contained many of his own choruses. In recent years, certain gospel songwriters, such as Wendell P. Loveless, Norman J. Clayton and Harry Dixon Loes, have also become known for their chorus writing.

b. The gospel "special," differing from the gospel song in that it is for solo, duet, trio, quartet or choir rather than for congregational singing. It is usually colorfully harmonized and written for certain occasions, or based on special themes, and is most frequently either an expression of personal fellowship with Christ or an appeal to others to receive him. This field contains many worthy compositions, such as "How Great Thou Art" (a translation from an old Swedish song), "It Took a Miracle" by John Peterson and "The Love of God" by F. M. Lehman.

RECOMMENDED READING

Foote, H. W. *Three Centuries of American Hymnody*. Hamden, Conn.: The Shoe String Press, 1961.

Ninde, E. S. *Nineteen Centuries of Christian Song*. Westwood, N.J.; Fleming H. Revell Co., 1938.

Swan, A. J. *The Music Director's Guide to Musical Literature*. New York: Prentice-Hall, Inc., 1941.

Sydnor, J. R. *The Hymn and Congregational Singing*. Richmond: John Knox Press, 1960.

Chapter 9

WAYS OF EVALUATING HYMNODY

Introduction

There are many important factors to be considered in seeking to gain an understanding of and appreciation for church hymnody. The accompanying evaluation chart has been designed to help the minister, church musician and layman gain an overall picture of the background, worth and usefulness of the hymnody found in the church hymnal. It is suggested that if several selections of contrasting styles and periods are evaluated in light of the categories given, a reasonable amount of skill will soon be developed in recognizing the strong and weak points in existing hymns, thus making it easier to select music for use in the church. The points of evaluation are based on three approaches: the statistical facts, an analytical study and a personal evaluation.

Statistical Evaluation

1. Name. The hymn is usually identified by the first line of the first stanza. However, some gospel songs have obtained other traditional titles based on a key phrase within their text or refrain. An example is "Near to the Heart of God" (McAfee). Still others have become identified by names which are not contained in the text, such as "My Prayer," otherwise recognized as "More Holiness Give Me" (P. P. Bliss).

2. Author. The writer of the words is referred to as the author. His name appears at the upper left of the hymn. When the words are translated from another language, it will be listed as follows:

Joachim Neander, 1650—1680 (the author)
Trans. by Catherine Winkworth (the translator)

If the words are taken from the Scriptures but are altered by an author, this will be identified in the following manner:

From Psalm 100
Ascribed to William Kethe, 16th century, alt.

111

"Alt." indicates that someone, perhaps the editors of the hymnal, altered the words of Kethe.

If the source of the words is unknown, this will be so indicated and will often be accompanied by the estimated *circa* date when written (c. 1757), or it will simply be marked "anon." meaning anonymous. Other hymns may be identified by the sources from whence they came, such as the *Scottish Psalter* or the **Foundling Hospital Collection**; or the original language may simply be indicated, as "from the Latin."

3. Date, era or movement. Most hymn texts should be identified by the years of birth and death of the author. Many can also be traced back to certain historical events, eras, movements or periods. These are based on the period studied in the preceding chapter.

4. Tune. Most hymn tunes have names which have been given to them by either the composer, the publisher or tradition. These are particularly necessary when identifying tunes which are associated with more than one set of words, such as Federal Street by Henry Oliver. This is associated with "God Calling Yet" (Terstee- gen-Borthwick), "Jesus, and Shall It Ever Be?" (Grigg-Francis) and "Great God, We Sing That Mighty Hand" (Doddridge).

5. Composer. The name of the writer of the music, known as the composer, appears at the upper right of the hymn. Sometimes the source of the tune is a collection, such as the Bohemian Breth- ren's *Gesangbuch* (songbook), or by a historical style or idiom, such as the Gregorian Chant. Tunes which have been harmonized, edited or arranged by another composer will show that information immediately below the composer's name.

6. Date and period. The identification of the date and period in which the music was written is particularly valuable when deter- mining the manner in which it should be performed. The skilled musician will understand the style of phrasing, the organ and vocal tone and the general manner of interpretation associated with the many periods of music literature represented in hymnody. As a re- sult, he will seek to execute each hymn in the manner most suitable to its style.

7. Meter. The metrical index found in the back of most hymnals indicates the number of word syllables provided for in the music. These are shown by numbers representing each of the phrases in the tune. As an example, the tune Mercy (arr. from Louis M. Gottschalk) is listed as 7,7,7,7; therefore it is possible to use it with the following words:

HYMN EVALUATION CHART

Statistics	Name and number		
	Author of text		
	Date, era or movement of text		
	Tune		
	Composer of music		
	Date and period of music		
	Meter		
Analysis	Scriptural source		
	Subject treated		
	To whom directed		
	Style		
Evaluation	Evaluation of text		
	Evaluation of music		
	Compatibility of text and music		
	Usage		
	Personal rating		
	Remarks		

Ho-ly Ghost, with light di-vine,   (7)
Shine up-on this heart of mine;   (7)
Chase the shades of night a-way,   (7)
Turn my dark-ness in-to day.   (7)

(Andrew Reed, 1817)

All the texts and tunes having the same meter are identified in the metrical index under the listing 7,7,7,7, thus making it easy to interchange tunes with other texts, thereby adding new interest to congregational singing. After checking the index, one will discover that the above words can also be sung to the tune Posen (Georg C. Strattner) or the Norwegian folk song "Kari." Three of the most frequently used meters are also known by the following names:

Common meter   (C.M.)   8,6,8,6.
                                  "Amazing Grace"

Long meter   (L.M.)   8,8,8,8.
                                  "When I Survey the Wondrous Cross"

Short meter   (S.M.)   6,6,8,6.
                                  "Blest Be the Tie That Binds"

Many of the meters are double in length, therefore are indicated as follows: 6,5,6,5, D; or in another instance simply C.M.D., indicating common meter (8,6,8,6) doubled.

Analytical Evaluation

1. Scripture source. Many hymn texts are based directly on Scripture verses or passages, some almost verbatim and others in content alone. "The Lord Is My Shepherd" is an almost verbatim adaptation of Psalm 23 by James Montgomery, while "Joy to the World," composed by Isaac Watts, is a very free treatment of the ideas prevalent in Psalm 98. Whereas many other hymns are not as closely related to scriptural passages, most of them are built around certain thoughts or doctrines which come from the Bible.

One such example is "The Church's One Foundation" (Stone), which must have been inspired by the verse: "Other foundation can no man lay than that is laid, which is Jesus Christ" (I Cor. 3:11). Another example is "Break Thou the Bread of Life" (Lathbury), based on the story of Christ breaking the loaves and feeding the five thousand (Matt. 14:15-21).

It is true that some hymn texts are only remotely connected with their Scripture sources, therefore it is difficult to identify them, yet it is important that this be done so that choices of hymns can be more systematic. Some hymnals have an index of Scripture sources at the back of the book to help the average church musician or pastor build a service of song around the pastor's message or central theme of the day.

2. Subject. Perhaps the most important factor to consider in evaluating a text is the subject matter treated. Some texts can be categorized in several ways, as will be observed in the topical index of a hymnal. For example, the hymn "All Hail the Power of Jesus' Name" (Edward Perronet) might be classified as a hymn based on the reign of Christ, the name of Christ, or the coming kingdom. Each of these categories helps determine the many possible usages of the hymn.

3. To whom directed. It is also important to determine the direction to which the text is pointed. Some texts are directed upward to the Godhead, such as:

"O God, Our Help in Ages Past" (Isaac Watts)
"Great Is Thy Faithfulness" (Thomas O. Chisholm)
"Jesus, Keep Me Near the Cross" (Fanny J. Crosby)
"Spirit of God, Descend Upon My Heart" (George Croly)

Others are directed outward to man, telling him about the Godhead or exhorting him to praise. Some examples are:

"What a Friend We Have in Jesus" (Joseph Scriven)
"O Worship the King" (Robert Grant)
"A Mighty Fortress Is Our God" (Martin Luther)

Still others are directed inward to the singer, usually intended for all people as well. These include:

"This Is My Father's World" (Maltbie D. Babcock)
"Alas, and Did My Saviour Bleed?" (Isaac Watts)

Many texts change their course of direction on certain stanzas. For example, the first two stanzas of the gospel song "He Leadeth Me" (Joseph H. Gilmore) are directed inward to the singer, but the last two point upward to the Lord. Also, "When I Survey the Wondrous Cross" (Isaac Watts), though directed inward, points upward in the second stanza, which reads "Forbid it, Lord, that I should boast, Save in the death of Christ, my God . . ."

Other categories to be considered are the people to whom the hymns are directed. "Give of Your Best to the Master" (Howard B. Grose) is directed to youth. "Let Jesus Come into Your Heart" (Lelia N. Morris) is a plea to the sinner. "Ye Christian Heralds" (Bourne H. Draper) is a challenge to the Christian worker. "Like a River Glorious" (Frances R. Havergal) is a message of comfort to the believer.

4. Style. It is sometimes hard to differentiate between the many styles of hymnody, but it is possible to make a general analysis

using classifications similar to those found in Colossians 3:16: psalms, hymns and spiritual (gospel) songs. Usually the text is the determining factor as to whether it should be classified as a psalm, a hymn or a gospel song. However, there are many instances where a hymn text or psalm setting has been placed into a gospel song musical setting, such as was done to the Isaac Watts text, "Alas, and Did My Saviour Bleed?" when Ralph E. Hudson added a refrain and composed a gospel song entitled "At the Cross."

Other than such exceptions, the following general rules can be established as ample for distinguishing the three styles:

The psalm is a hymn-style composition containing words taken directly from the Psalms. This would include:

"All People That on Earth Do Dwell" (Psalm 100)

"The Lord's My Shepherd" (Psalm 23)

The hymn text is of human design and is expressive of praise, adoration or supplication. It is either directed to God or about God. Several types of hymns would include:

"My Faith Looks Up to Thee" (Ray Palmer)

"Faith of Our Fathers" (Frederick W. Faber)

"Blest Be the Tie That Binds" (John Fawcett)

The gospel song text contains a testimony of fellowship with Christ or a personal experience related to the Christian life. This includes all three types previously discussed: the congregational gospel song, the chorus and the gospel song special.

Personal Evaluation

This aspect of the evaluation gives opportunity for personal opinion.

1. Evaluation of text. To evaluate a text properly, one must observe three things:

a. Its content. Is the text in keeping with biblical truths and sound doctrines? Is the message clearly portrayed?

b. Its style of writing. Is it good poetry? Does it have consistency of thought?

c. Its word usage. Is it picturesque and descriptive, yet without an overuse of superlatives and symbolisms?

2. Evaluation of music. The musical content should be that of well-constructed melody accompanied by consistent harmonies and rhythms, blended together in a uniform manner.

3. Compatibility of text and music. It is possible for a hymn to have both a good text and well-constructed music yet still not be a good hymn. The vital factor is the compatibility of text and music. Unless the music provides a strong vehicle for interpretation of the text, it will not adequately fulfill its function.

4. *Usage.* The way in which a hymn can be used depends largely upon the points found in the analytical evaluation. The personal evaluation of its usage, however, more specifically refers to the type of public service in which it can be used, the position it may take within the service, the season of the year in which it is best suited for use, and the special ministries which it is able to perform. As contrasting examples, "Crown Him with Many Crowns" (Bridges-Thring) may be used as an opening hymn of praise, or as a processional, and is especially suited for Ascension Sunday; whereas "More Love to Thee" (Elizabeth P. Prentiss) is effective as a hymn of devotion and may be used preceding prayer, or as a song of dedication and commitment following the sermon.

5. *Personal rating.* A well-chosen hymn will not be one which merely meets the minimum requirements in standards and usefulness; rather it will, in the opinion of the selector, meet all the requirements in the most satisfactory way possible. In order to determine this, it is a good practice to rate all the hymns evaluated in light of the results of the evaluation. A suggested plan is to classify them in five divisions: (1) superior, (2) very useful, (3) useful, but with certain limitations, (4) weak, (5) not worthy of consideration.

6. *Remarks.* Any further comments which will help recall the findings of the evaluation should be noted for future reference. This will frequently be nothing more than a brief summary of the findings.

Conclusion

It has been previously stated that the minister, the church musician and the layman should each become thoroughly acquainted with the contents of his own church hymnal. Some seminaries are now requiring all pastoral candidates to complete a study and evaluation of each hymn in the denominational hymnal before graduating. This is a tried and proved way of fostering greater interest in learning new hymns and of placing increased importance upon hymn singing as an integral part of worship. It is also a vital asset in building the future minister's vocabulary, as well as an aid to his ability of expressing himself more fluently. On the other hand, the experience of learning and appraising hymns provides the layman and the church musician with new opportunities to study and understand theology and Christian doctrines.

RECOMMENDED READING

BAILEY, A. E. *The Gospel in Hymns.* New York: Charles Scribner's Sons, 1950.

BLACKWOOD, A. W. *The Fine Art of Public Worship.* Nashville: Abingdon Press, 1934.

FARLANDER, A. W. *The Hymnal: How to Use It.* New York: Protestant Episcopal Church, 1951. Pamphlet.

RYDEN, E. E. *The Story of Christian Hymnody.* Rock Island, Ill.: Augustana Book Concern, 1959.

Chapter 10

CONGREGATIONAL SINGING

Introduction

Congregational singing is a distinctive of the Protestant church. It was reborn with the Reformation and is described by Ashton as "the basic form of Protestant church music."[1] However, it is not an invention of the Reformation but rather the restoration of a biblically ordained medium through which to worship.

Its Effectiveness in the Past

While David's psalms encourage all men to praise the Lord with singing, no evidence has ever been found wherein the congregation sang as a part of worship during his day. Nearly all accounts of temple worship indicate that the singing was done only by "the singers with instruments of musick, and such as taught to sing praise" (II Chron. 23:13), "as it was ordained by David" (v. 18), referring to his appointed musicians found in I Chronicles 15:17.

The earlier psalms were written by David specifically for the chief musicians, and were delivered into their hands (I Chron. 16:7) to be sung by their choirs. Other psalms were either authored or collected by the musicians Asaph, Heman and Ethan, presumably for the same purpose. On the other hand, the later psalms, especially beginning with Psalm 92, seem to place a definite emphasis upon the participation of all the people in song. "Sing unto the Lord, all the earth" (Ps. 96:1). This suggests that congregational singing must have developed some time after the temple worship patterns had been set by the Levitical choirs. The book of Psalms is believed to have been used as a hymnal in the second temple, and the structure of many of the psalms indicates that they might have been sung antiphonally between the choir and the people.

The New Testament gives many indications of the practice of

---

[1] J. N. Ashton, *Music in Worship* (Boston: Pilgrim Press, 1943), p. 92.

congregational singing, as is evidenced by Christ and his disciples when they met for the Last Supper, by Paul when he admonished the churches at Corinth, Ephesus and Colosse to sing with grace in their hearts to the Lord, and by James when he suggested that men should sing when merry.

Whatever had been developed in the way of congregational singing virtually gave way to choirs in the early Christian church, and was not fully regained until the time when Luther made it possible for the entire congregation to join in the singing at the services.

John Wesley gave much prominence to it in his services during the English Reformation, often preaching on the "duty and privilege of congregational singing." He also wrote seven "rules for the singers," which condemned slow singing as a "drawling way" which "naturally steals on all who are lazy."

Its Ministry Today

To participate in congregational singing is both a privilege and a responsibility of the man in the pew. Yet its real values will not be known until he first learns to understand the text, and then feels the inspiration of the text and the music together. "I will sing with the spirit, and I will sing with the understanding also" (I Cor. 14:15). In writing to the churches at Ephesus and Colosse, Paul developed a threefold function of music which applies to the ministry of congregational singing:

1. It is ingoing. "Speaking to yourselves in psalms and hymns and spiritual songs" (Eph. 5:19). The most vital ministry of singing is to the person himself. Whether or not he is capable of singing with musical finesse, he can find truths in the texts which comfort, challenge, chasten, and even change his life.

2. Congregational singing is up-reaching. "Singing with grace in your hearts to the Lord" (Col. 3:16). The hymn serves as a means of helping man with his stammering tongue express himself to God. The words, though written by another, can become the individual's own expression of worship, praise, supplication or dedication.

3. Congregational singing is outgoing. "Teaching and admonishing one another in psalms and hymns and spiritual songs" (Col. 3:16). A person's presence and participation in song serve as a testimony to others. Together with the rest of the congregation, he is able to proclaim the doctrines of God to those around him and to admonish them to walk in the ways of truth. This was so apparent in

the days of the Reformation that one of Luther's critics exclaimed, "The whole people are singing itself into the Lutheran doctrine."

The Necessity for Leadership

In the early nonliturgical churches in America, a precentor was used to direct the psalmody. He would probably compare with what is often referred to as a song leader today. When the European churches used the congregation to sing the hymns and parts of their liturgy, the organist assumed leadership with his instrument. In other instances the pastor or rector would announce the hymns and assume a certain amount of direction over the singing. It is difficult to determine who should be given the responsibility of congregational leadership in song, as it is conceivable that any of the three might be found effective, but perhaps under differing circumstances. In order to determine this, the following factors must be considered:

1. The message of the hymn. Hymns such as "Our God, Our Help in Ages Past" (St. Anne), "O Master, Let Me Walk with Thee" (Maryton) or "Spirit of God, Descend upon My Heart" (Morecambe) are designed to draw a person into deep inner thought, in an experience of personal communion between himself and God. Human directorship can become a distraction, and even the pastor or leader of the service must be careful not to do anything that will draw attention from this act of interfellowship with God. Leadership from the organ is less personal and will guide the singing without diverting the worshiper's attention.

On the other hand, gospel songs with messages of testimony or personal challenge, such as "Blessed Assurance" (Knapp), "What a Friend We Have in Jesus" (Converse) and "Stand Up, Stand Up for Jesus" (Webb) are designed to draw all persons together as a corporate body to share experiences. The presence of a song leader will often contribute to this feeling of unity, and thus make the singing experience more meaningful.

2. The nature of the music. Because of their musical structure, some gospel songs require leadership. This is especially true of those with frequent rhythm and tempo changes, or with occasional fermatas, such as "He Leadeth Me" (Bradbury), "Faith Is the Victory" (Sankey) and "Jesus Is All the World to Me" (Thompson). Others, such as "The Church's One Foundation" (Aurelia) and "Sweet Hour of Prayer" (Bradbury) can be sung adequately with direction from the organ or indication from the leader of worship.

3. The service. A song leader is essential in gatherings where the foremost emphasis is placed on informal fellowship in song. He must then announce the hymns and perhaps emphasize briefly their relationship to the service or direct the congregation to the message they contain. The service which is directed toward worship and praise, provided the hymn numbers are clearly indicated in an order of worship or displayed on a hymn board, is not as dependent upon human leadership.

4. The sanctuary and the instrument. Many times physical factors make it mandatory to use a song leader at all services and for all hymns. If the sanctuary is very long and wide, if acoustical problems make it difficult to clearly hear the organ, or if the organ itself is inadequate, the church is wise to employ a director for the congregational singing.

Responsibilities of the Leadership

While the nature of the responsibilities may vary according to the situation, the song leader, organist and pastor are all vital to the ministry of congregational singing. Their areas of leadership should include the following:

1. The song leader. The song leader must realize that there is a time to direct and a time to participate. Where his conducting will be an asset in one instance, it may be a detriment in another.

a. The song leader is able to make the following important contributions to the singing:

(1) The announcing of hymn numbers, clarification of stanzas to be used or omitted, and instructions concerning rising and sitting.

(2) The focusing of the singers' attention upon the basic thought found in the hymn; for example, introducing it as "a hymn of majestic praise to God" or "a song of comfort and assurance."

(3) The inspiring of a better response in singing by exhibiting an attitude which projects the nature of the hymn.

(4) The setting of correct tempi, dynamics and contrasts through his conducting.

(5) The showing of definite attacks, releases, fermatas and tempo changes.

(6) The instilling of confidence in the congregation by appearing poised and confident himself.

(7) The correlating of the congregational singing to the rest of the service, by brief comments and proper attitudes and by preparing the people for that which is to follow.

b. Things the song leader must avoid:

(1) Talking too much. Brief phrases or sentences will usually be sufficient to accomplish any of the above.

(2) Giving the impression that loudness and speed are synonymous with good singing. He should strive rather for dignity and majesty, brightness and spiritual joy, or other mood ideas which relate to the particular textual content.

(3) Scolding or showing an attitude of dissatisfaction.

(4) The use of "gymnastics," distracting jokes or stories.

(5) An apologetic approach.

2. *The organist.* Right or wrong, the organist is the actual leader of the congregation. A capable song leader is rendered almost helpless unless the organist is sensitive to his direction, since the congregation will usually respond to that which is heard instead of that which is seen.

a. The following five rules should be followed by the organist—or the pianist, with minor adaptations—when playing for a congregation, with or without a song leader.

(1) Determine the nature of the first stanza of the hymn and prepare the stops accordingly. Stop combinations should lend good support to the singing, but should never be too imposing or shrill. The degree of strength and the type of color desired will depend on the hymn being used, the size of the congregation, the size of the auditorium and the acoustics.

(2) Prepare at least two contrasting stop combinations to be used for other stanzas.

(3) Observe the tempo and dynamics needed (or desired by the leader), and play the introduction exactly as the first stanza should be sung. If the hymn is quite lengthy, it may be best to play only a portion of it, ending on a complete cadence which will clearly establish the key and the beginning note of the melody.

(4) Lead the congregation throughout (observing the directions of the leader), rather than hesitating until they begin. This does not mean to keep ahead of them, but rather to play with the assumption that they are dependent upon the accompanist to both set and maintain the tempo.

(5) Maintain a steady rhythm within the natural phrases of the hymn, but provide ample time for breathing between phrases. It is advisable to develop the habit of "breathing with the congregation" at these places, so that the size of the breaks will be consistent.

b. The organist must be careful to avoid:

(1) Too much use of vibrato or tremulant; they diminish the strength in sound, create an uncertainty of pitch and a lack of rhythmic support. Most hymns will sound better without any at all.

(2) Monotony caused by lack of variety in stop combinations, excess volume or too little, too much unbroken legato playing, little or no change in volume.

(3) Excess variety, caused by sudden changes of stops, constant manipulation of expression pedal, erratic phrasing.

3. The pastor. Whether or not he leads the singing, the pastor holds several keys to the success of congregational worship through singing. These are especially felt in the following two areas:

a. The selection of hymns. When he selects them himself, the pastor is usually very much aware of textual contents and their appropriateness to the message of the hour. It is possible, however, that he will need to consult with the minister of music or organist to determine whether or not the music is also fitting, and the text and the music are properly suited one to the other. It is also conceivable that he will need to be careful to avoid an overemphasis or repetition of thought in the hymns he selects.

If, however, the hymns are chosen by the song leader, the pastor can help him by indicating the nature of hymns he feels would be desirable, or by suggesting a thematic treatment which could be followed in making the choices.

b. Placing proper emphasis on the value of congregational singing. In the days of John Wesley and Jonathan Edwards, ministers frequently devoted sermons to the importance and significance of music. While it is not necessary for a pastor to do this, he should help the cause of developing more meaningful singing by verbally stressing its values from time to time, by giving this ministry its proper place among the many other ministries of the church, and by displaying an obvious interest by entering into the fellowship of song himself.

Preparing for Congregational Singing

1. Choosing the hymns. Certain criteria should be considered when choosing the hymns for congregational singing. These include:

a. The worthiness of each hymn. That the hymn may make the greatest contribution possible, it must be worthy of use. Its worthiness can best be determined by evaluating the text, music and compatibility of both, in the manner suggested in the hymn evaluation chart in Chapter 9. Care must be taken to avoid texts which include confusing terminologies, questionable theological implications, or trite expressions and symbolisms. In addition to this, the music must give proper expression of the text without oversentimentalizing or overdramatizing its meaning.

b. Musical variety. A good balance of tempi, dynamics and styles of music is essential, not only for stimulating general interest but also for assuring better communication with the people.

c. Familiarity. Another important means of communication is through the well-known and well-loved hymns. Every service should include hymns which are familiar to the congregation.

d. Challenge. Along with the singing of the familiar hymns should be the ever-present challenge of learning new ones, thus increasing the congregation's repertoire of hymnody and thereby broadening its scope of worship.

e. Balance of types of hymns used. Apparently the Apostle Paul wished to stress the differences between the "psalms, hymns and spiritual songs" (Col. 3:16) when writing to the church at Colosse. These three categorical divisions suggest the balance of types of hymns which should be used in the church services. No service would be complete without:

(1) The ministries of praise such as are found in the psalms and hymns addressed to the Godhead.

(2) The ministries of prayer, supplication and dedication, found in the hymns of more devotional and personal content.

(3) The ministries of personal expression, as found in gospel songs and hymns of testimony and personal experience.

It is to be noted that these three ministries correspond with the ingoing, up-reaching and outgoing ministries previously mentioned.

2. Planning the service. While much of the planning of the service is dependent upon the choosing of the hymns, it is also important that the order, or structure, of the service be carefully outlined. The following steps should prove helpful:

a. Begin the service by using hymns which direct attention to the Godhead, either in an act of reverence, an expression of praise, or a testimony to the goodness of God, the provision of salvation made by Christ, the work and power of the Holy Spirit.

b. Include hymns that teach and admonish.

c. Select hymns that prepare hearts for prayer, the reading of. Scripture, the presentation of the message. These should be strategically placed so that they build up to these important parts of the service.

d. Conclude the service with a hymn geared to provoke a per-

TYPE OF HYMN USED	WORSHIP SERVICE	EVANGELISTIC CRUSADE	MISSIONARY CONFERENCE	YOUTH RALLY	CHILDREN'S MEETING
Worship and praise to the Godhead	All Hail the Power (Perronet-Holden) Come, Thou Almighty King (Anon.-Giardini) All Creatures of Our God and King (Draper-German)	Praise Him, Praise Him (Crosby-Allen) Blessed Assurance (Crosby-Knapp) To God Be the Glory (Crosby-Doane)	Jesus Shall Reign (Watts-Hatton) Christ for the World! We Sing (Wolcott-Giardini) In Christ There Is No East or West (Oxenham-Reinagle)	Rejoice, Ye Pure in Heart (Plumptre-Messiter) He Keeps Me Singing (Bridgers) Oh, How I Love Jesus (Whitfield-Anon.)	Fairest Lord Jesus (17th cent.-Willis) That Beautiful Name (Perry-Camp) For the Beauty of the Earth (Pierpoint-Kocher)
Teaching and admonishing	The Church's One Foundation (Stone-Wesley) Jesus! Engrave It on My Heart (Medley-Elvey) O God, Our Help in Ages Past (Watts-Croft)	Arise, My Soul, Arise (Wesley-Anon.) I Know Whom I Have Believed (Whittle-McGranahan) Our Great Saviour (Chapman-Pritchard)	The Call for Reapers (Thompson-Clemm) Send the Light (Gabriel) From Greenland's Icy Mountains (Heber-Mason)	Give of Your Best to the Master (Grose-Barnard) Grace Greater Than All Our Sin (Johnston-Towner) He Leadeth Me (Gilmore-Bradbury)	This Is My Father's World (Babcock-Sheppard) I Think When I Read That Sweet Story (Luke-Bradbury) Nothing but the Blood (Lowry)
Preparation of hearts for prayer, Scripture, message	I Want a Principle Within (Wesley-Spohr) Jesus, the Very Thought of Thee (Clairvaux-Dykes) Holy Ghost, with Light Divine (Reed-Gottschalk)	More about Jesus (Hewitt-Sweney) Revive Us Again (Mackay-Husband) Near the Cross (Crosby-Doane)	Beneath the Cross of Jesus (Clephane-Maker) Am I a Soldier of the Cross? (Watts-Arne) A Passion for Souls (Tovey-Fellers)	Open My Eyes, That I May See (Scott) Saviour, Like A Shepherd Lead Us (Thrupp-Bradbury) Take Time to Be Holy (Longstaff-Stebbins)	Tell Me the Story of Jesus (Crosby-Sweney) Thy Word Have I Hid in My Heart (Sellers) Holy Bible, Book Divine (Burton-Bradbury)
Provoking a personal commitment	My Jesus, As Thou Wilt (Borthwick-VonWeber) All for Jesus (James-Stainer) O for a Closer Walk with God (Cowper-Dykes)	Only Trust Him (Stockton) Whiter Than Snow (Nicholson-Fischer) O Jesus, Thou Art Standing (How-Husband)	Take My Life, and Let It Be (Havergal-Malan) Bring Them In (Thomas-Ogden) O Zion, Haste (Thomson-Walch)	I Would Be True (Walter-Peek) Lead On, O King Eternal (Shurtleff-Smart) Oh, to Be Like Thee (Chisholm-Kirkpatrick)	Jesus Bids Us Shine (Warner-Excell) Onward, Christian Soldiers (Baring-Gould-Sullivan) In Our Work and in Our Play (Wills-English)

sonal commitment, usually based on the message or the emphasis of the hour. This will include such personal aspects as dedication, salvation, challenge for service, trust and confidence in God.

It is to be noted that the above steps can be adapted to many kinds of services, including worship services, evangelistic crusades, missionary conferences, youth rallies and children's meetings. The accompanying chart gives examples of hymns which may be used on these varied occasions.

Preparing the Congregation *read 127-128*

There are many ways by which the man in the pew can be prepared to enjoy more fully and participate more actively in congregational singing. Even though he may be unschooled in the fundamentals of music, note reading and singing techniques, he can be taught to appreciate this time of singing and to see in it an unmatched opportunity for communing with God, as well as a means of spiritual growth and personal expression. He can also be made to realize its potential as a Christian ministry to those around him. However, these attitudes are seldom developed without some help from the leadership of the church. There are many ways in which this can be done.

1. Through adult education. As has been mentioned before, Wesley and Edwards preached sermons on the ministry of participation in singing. Today, certain denominations and churches are conducting organized classes and programs to develop an appreciation of hymn singing and worship among their church members. Some pastors have prepared series of sermons on these and related subjects, or have devoted time during their midweek Bible study and prayer meetings to broaden the layman's knowledge of hymnody. All these contribute to the overall Christian testimony and experience of the adult members of the church, and therefore are worthwhile endeavors to consider.

2. Through Christian education activities. The graded choirs, youth fellowships, children's organizations and other educational programs can be geared toward training the children and youth to see the implications in worship through singing, or by conducting classes and discussions on related subjects. The Sunday school and children's church can also follow a regular program of learning hymns, such as has been outlined in the chapter on Christian education.

3. Through interchurch hymn festivals and workshops. The limitations of the small church often make the above mentioned edu-

cation classes impractical. Therefore, many Bible colleges, denominations and local ministerial groups have provided interchurch conferences, lectures and workshops to challenge and train lay people for various phases of church and Sunday school responsibilities. These media may also be used to promote and develop better hymn singing, as well as to train song leaders and accompanists.

Practical Factors Relating to Congregational Singing

There are many small but important factors which must be considered in making congregational singing an effective act of worship. They include:

1. An adequate supply of good hymnals. A general rule would be to provide at least one hymnal for every two people, easily accessible to their pews. The quality and the condition of the hymnal are also important.

2. Standing position while singing. The unwritten rule of worship is to stand when singing, kneel when praying, sit when listening. In most instances it is best to have the congregation stand while singing; however, if there is to be a prolonged period of singing, or if the congregation includes many elderly people, it may be wise to take exception to this rule on occasion. In such cases, the quiet hymns of inner reflection and meditation may be sung while seated. The leader should be clear and explicit when signaling the congregation to rise and sit, using an extended arm gesture similar to that used by a choir director.

3. Good lighting, ventilation and heating. Comfort is an important commodity in conducting a church service, especially if the congregation is expected to participate actively. Poor lighting will cause a feeling of depression; and lack of ventilation, too much or too little heat will cause discomfort and often drowsiness.

Summary and Conclusion

Educational statistics claim that an average person retains only 10 percent of what he hears, but 90 percent of what he does. This suggests very clearly the value of worship in which the layman takes active part, as opposed to a completely passive (or spectator) type. Congregational singing is one of the most effective means of creating activity in worship, as well as promoting unity of thought among the worshipers and unanimity of spirit between the people in the pews. For these reasons, it should continue to be a basic part of all of the public services of the church, working hand in hand with the other ministries of song, but never replaced by them.

RECOMMENDED READING

ASHTON, J. N. *Music in Worship*. Boston: Pilgrim Press, 1943.

BACON, A. *The True Function of Church Music*. Stockton, Calif.: Printwell Press, 1953.

EISENBERG, H. and L. *How to Lead Group Singing*. New York: Association Press, 1955.

NININGER, R. *Growing a Musical Church*. Nashville: Broadman Press, 1947.

URANG, G. *Church Music—For the Glory of God*. Moline, Ill.: Christian Service Foundation, 1956.

WILSON, H. R., and LYALL, J. L. *Building a Church Choir*. Minneapolis: Hall and McCreary Co., 1957.

Chapter 11

THE GRADED CHOIR PROGRAM

Introduction

The graded choir system is that part of the church music program which provides the lifeblood of the organization. It consists of a series of choirs for all ages from early childhood through adulthood, ideally with no break in the sequence. Its functions are to train for the future while ministering to the present, to build future leaders for the church by making them leaders today, and to teach the values of service by permitting individuals to serve.

Its Background

The graded choir principle is not a new thing. From the very beginning of history we have evidence of training programs which were conducted in music. In Genesis 4:21, Jubal is identified as the "father of all such as handle the harp and organ." Although we know little more than the fact that he instructed in these instruments, we do have much more detailed evidence concerning the programs that followed, especially during the time of David.

1. *The temple music program.* Choir training programs of a graded nature have been in existence as far back as the time when the ark of the covenant was brought into Jerusalem and temple worship was established (I Chron. 23). At that time there were thirty-eight thousand Levites who were aged thirty and above, the age associated with the "service of the ministry" (Num. 4). Immediately after Solomon was made king, David assigned these Levites to various responsibilities in relation to the work of the temple. From this organizational move, the following three-point musical program was developed:

a. From the thirty-eight thousand, David appointed four thousand as musicians, who were to sing and play the instruments of David (I Chron. 15:16; 23-5).

b. Their sons who were twenty years and above worked with them as "apprentices" (23:24).

c. Heman, Asaph and Jeduthun, the chief musicians, were appointed to train 288 children "in the songs of the Lord, even all that were cunning" (25:6, 7), preparing them for future service in the temple.

In the years to come, these children were to step into the positions held by the fathers, thus carrying on the program to another generation. The results of this training program were still in evidence during the post-Exilic period more than four hundred and fifty years later, when the sons of Asaph were continuing the ministry as chief musicians (Neh. 11:22).

2. *The choir school.* The Christian church began conducting similar programs as early as the time of Pope Sylvester (314-335). St. Sylvester established a school of song in Rome to provide for the rapid increase in new church music, and to teach memorization, breathing and correct singing techniques. Since that time, the choir school has become prominent in the history of the church and includes, among others, the Schola Cantorium, attributed to Pope Gregory (sixth century), St. Thomas School of Leipzig, established in 1212 and later conducted by J. S. Bach, the Dresden Cross Choir, organized before the fourteenth century, and the Vienna Boys' Choir, founded in 1498 and still in existence.

Later English schools, such as those at Westminster Abbey and St. Paul's Cathedral, were the influences behind the establishing of the first American choir schools by the Protestant Episcopal churches of America. The earlier American schools included those at the Cathedral of St. Peter and St. Paul in Chicago (whose school was organized in 1870, but destroyed one year later by the Chicago fire), St. Paul's Parish of Baltimore (1870) and Grace Church in New York (1894).

Choir schools were originally designed to train the carefully selected boys who were to sing soprano and alto in the cathedral choir. After they had received about eight years of training and experience, they were usually ready to be promoted to the tenor and bass sections.

However, in 1946 a new type of choir school was organized at the First Lutheran Church of Rockford, Illinois, open to both boys and girls, and without regard to musical ability. This marked the beginning of a new music program which has spread all over the country, particularly among Lutheran churches.

3. *The multiple choir program.* Similarly influenced by the European choir school tradition, the multiple choir program came into existence sometime near the turn of the century, and is fast

becoming a vital part of the music program in all denominations. Although it has not replaced the traditional choir, many churches who utilize men's and boys' choirs have developed an additional training program for their girls, using them in services which are not confined to the liturgies.

For all practical purposes, the multiple choir program and the graded choir system are synonymous, and are both structured in the same way. The structure of the graded system is described in detail in chapter 5.

Building a Graded Choir Program

Ideally, one will begin with the complete system when starting a program in the church. This is not always practical, however, because of the number of members or the personnel required. The following is a suggested three-phase plan which will extend over a period of about four years:

1. First phase—two choirs

Juniors: ages 7 - 11 or grades 2 - 6. One can be assured of an enthusiastic response to an interesting program during this age span when the child's learning power is at its highest.

Adult: ages 15 and above. Under proper leadership, this combined span of youth and adults can become a very effective group.

It is seldom advisable to organize a new choir with ages 12 to 14 unless the youth have had some previous music background. During the first phase, these children should be encouraged to study music and participate in music in the youth groups or clubs. Or they may be incorporated into an instrumental ensemble, training class or handbell choir.

2. Second phase (one or two years after the inauguration of the first phase)—three choirs developed from the two:

Elementary	ages 7 - 9	or	grades 2 - 4
Intermediate	ages 10 - 14	or	grades 5 - 9
Adult	ages 15 and above		

It should be noted that the new intermediate choir will be made up of nearly half of those who were in the first phase junior choir, while the elementary choir will retain the other half. The latter may also drop the age to 6 if desirable.

3. Third phase (two years later)

The addition of a high school choir, or a redevelopment of the groups into one of the complete choir programs.

Choir Names

The impersonal nature of the classifications referred to above makes it advisable to consider interesting titles for each choir. Although there are many others that can be used, the names Celestial, Cherub, Carol, Concord, Chapel, Chancel and Cathedral (with respect to the complete system mentioned in chapter 5) are commonly accepted.

Organization

A well organized choir system has a program designed progressively from the bottom to the top, in which each choir serves as a preparation for the next one in sequence. To do this, while at the same time maintaining individual goals and approaches, takes capable leadership.

The leaders in the graded choir program are the minister of music, the choir sponsors or officers and the pastor, with the minister of music serving as the coordinator of all activities. In planning and scheduling rehearsals and special programs, he works with the director of Christian education, so that the plans will not conflict with activities in the Sunday school and other youth and adult organizations.

When there are several choirs in the system, the directing is often handled by one or two others in addition to the minister of music. They work in conjunction with the minister of music in maintaining a well-balanced program of activities for all groups.

The choir sponsors and officers assist the directors by caring for the attendance records each week, and in planning special membership drives, social functions and other activities. (See chapter 5.)

Membership

Membership in the children's choirs and youth choirs should be open to all. Christian experience and musicianship should not be prerequisites, since these constitute the spiritual ministry and musical challenge of this phase of the music program. On the other hand, the adult choir should have careful restrictions in regard to both Christian experience and musicianship. These will be discussed more fully in Chapter 13.

Acceptance into membership of all choirs should be preceded by:

1. An audition with the director to determine musical ability (junior and above).

2. The promise of good attendance and conduct for the entire year.

3. A designation of time for regular attendance before being officially inducted into the membership.

Auditions for children should be designed only to determine musical ability and background, not to eliminate those who are lacking in talent and training. Children with extreme vocal or pitch difficulties should be advised of their problems and, if necessary, restricted from public participation until these are remedied. In the meantime the director should seek to help them overcome the deficiencies.

Membership restrictions may need to be made if the choir program is attracting active churchgoers from neighboring churches; otherwise poor interchurch relations may result.

The Ministry of Children's and Youth Choirs

Although there is a certain phase of their ministry which reaches out into the home of each child who takes part, and there is great spiritual blessing received through listening to the singing of these groups, the primary ministry of the children's and youth choirs is to reach the ones who take part. In this way their objectives parallel those of the entire church, including the Sunday school and youth programs.

The following is a listing of the goals set forth by the graded choir system:

1. To evangelize. Every child who takes part in a church choir is presented with another opportunity of learning about Christ's message of redemption. This enhances the work which is being carried on simultaneously by the Sunday school and the church, and can often be the key to the child's receiving Christ into his life. For this reason the unchurched child or youth is encouraged to participate, as long as he is willing to meet the attendance requirements and the standards of conduct set forth by the organization. The choir not only brings the youth into the church but also enlarges the possibility of his family attending the services when his group sings. It often provides the initial contact of the church with the home, and frequently leads to further ministries. Therefore, the evangelistic outreach is to the entire family.

2. To teach worship. Worship must be learned and practiced before it can be fully experienced. A choir program can be used to teach the child to respect God and to be silent when in His presence. It can provide him with proper training in the disciplines of worship, its hymnody and its order. It can help him see the reason behind the various acts of worship, to know what to do during the many phases of the worship service, as well as what

they should do for him. All this will be learned in the rehearsals and put to practice in the services in which he sings.

3. To foster spiritual growth. The two necessary substances of spiritual growth are worshiping God and studying His Word. Through the wise guidance of a spiritually minded director and a careful choice of repertoire, a choir program offers its young members great opportunities to learn the doctrines and truths found in the Word of God. The fact that they must not only sing but also interpret the texts helps them to become more aware of the messages found within. In addition to this, the music serves as a most powerful tool of interpretation and recall. The constant repetition in rehearsal plus the requirements of memorization help to implant a message within the members' minds which will never be lost. An acceptance of the truths which have been so forcefully impressed upon them through this process will in turn develop into spiritual growth and maturity.

4. To give opportunity for Christian service. One of the most unique aspects of the entire church music ministry is its emphasis on Christian service, another necessary substance of spiritual growth. Every time a choir sings, each member becomes a minister of the gospel. He is thereby presenting a message which may meet the need of someone in the congregation or in the choir, besides meeting his own need.

This opportunity brings with it great responsibilities as well. The member's presence, his attitude, the way he sings and the way he stands all contribute to the conveyance of or distraction from the message. Therefore he is important as an individual while he is part of a group.

His attitudes toward the Christian ministry will usually have a lasting effect upon his future service to the Lord and in His church. The choir program can help him realize the seriousness of the task of service as well as impress on him the joys of being a servant. It can also show him the potentials of service, especially if he is able to witness visible results coming from the choir ministry of which he is a part. It may very well result in the beginning of a life of service to the Lord as a pastor, missionary or Christian layman.

5. To provide Christian fellowship. The companionship found in a choir can help mold the life of the child or young person. The organized activities deter from other less desirable activities and associations, and at the same time center the member's social life around the church. In a day when children of all ages are faced

with almost insurmountable temptations, the choirs give them two of the strongest allies they can find: fellowship and companionship with individuals who will in turn strengthen each other in the faith.

RECOMMENDED READING

INGRAM, M. *Organizing and Directing Children's Choirs.* Nashville: Abingdon Press, 1959.

JACOBS, R. K. *The Successful Children's Choir.* Chicago: H. T. FitzSimons, 1948.

LUNDSTROM, L. J. *The Choir School.* Minneapolis: Augsburg Publishing House, 1957.

MILLER, P. J. *Youth Choirs.* New York: Harold Flammer, Inc., 1953.

Chapter 12

METHODS

Children's and Youth Choirs — Introduction

The methods and materials used in each of the choral groups are quite varied. It is necessary to determine the characteristics and learning ability of each age and the goal of achievement desired, before deciding upon the materials to be used.

The following pages outline a program which is founded on the commonly accepted levels of child development and maturity. Due to the fact that the program is based upon typical school standards and on family, social, regional and environmental influences, it may need to be adjusted accordingly. If this is so, the structure should remain the same, but the apportionment of materials would need to be altered.

The program is also based on the assumption that most of the choir members have benefited from the materials used in the previous groups. When such is not the case, it will be necessary to begin with many of the basic fundamentals initiated in the primary choir, adapting them to the age level.

Preschool, Ages 3-5

Rehearsal time: approximately 20 minutes.

1. Characteristics. Learning is accomplished by rote (imitating the teacher), and is best administered in small groups. Attention control is short, particularly in larger groups. Music potential is very small, since pitch sense, rhythm and coordination need to be developed. Memorization is accomplished easily, but things are forgotten just as quickly. Repetition is essential to both learning and retaining. Imagination and creativity are high.

2. Rehearsal goals. To teach the child to sit, stand and act like a good choir member. To teach him to listen and to learn. To establish rhythmic pulses and pitch sense. To teach him simple truths concerning Jesus' love, the aspects of God's nature (trees, flowers, birds, animals, and seeds which grow).

3. Rehearsal activities

a. Rhythm bands using toy drums and other percussion instruments, kitchen utensils, wooden sticks, bells and toy horns. A child conductor may lead with a baton, and an adult pianist or phonograph recording may play while instruments keep time. Do not use complex rhythms, just basic beats.

b. Marching drills, with children marching or marking time while pianist or phonograph plays songs in 4/4 time. Children can also sing familiar songs in this manner.

c. Matching of pitches, with children imitating vocally the assorted pitches and short musical phrases played by pianist or sung by director.

4. Repertoire. Music should consist of simple children's songs involving short phrases, vocal ranges of about an octave (*d* to *d*) and steady rhythms preferably with motions describing the text. Piano accompaniments should be flowing in style but must support the voices. Texts should be direct and should not involve complex words or long phrases.

5. Performances. This is not primarily a performing group, but the rhythm band could be used occasionally in Sunday school or in Children's Day programs, and singing could be done along with several other children's choirs.

Primary, Ages 6-8 or Grades 1-3

Rehearsal time: from 30 to 45 minutes.

1. Characteristics. Learning is still accomplished by rote, but reading is to be encouraged. Attention span has increased greatly. Music potential is good, especially along lines of basic fundamentals; however, pitch difficulties are quite prevalent. Memorization comes easily and retention is improving. Repetition is essential but can occur in larger intervals. Discipline is being learned in school and response to instruction is very good. Small responsibilities are readily accepted when they are clearly defined and supervised. Learning is best accomplished in groups, but some children need the challenge of individual projects in addition to group activity. A few are taking music lessons. Imagination and creativity are still high.

2. Rehearsal goals. To teach good posture, procedures for lining up and processing. To train in listening habits, to recognize themes, dynamic changes and pitches. To teach music fundamentals, note values, rhythm patterns and pitch perception. To acquaint with the piano keyboard. To develop pure vocal tones. To teach worship habits, easy hymnody and basic truths about attitudes concerning worship, love for God, how to be obedient and how to do good.

3. Rehearsal activities

a. Vocalizations: singing sequences of the vowel syllables, "Ya,ha,ha,ha,ha," "Yo,ho,ho,ho,ho," and "Yoo,hoo,hoo,hoo,hoo," on a major broken chord pattern, beginning on middle *c* and going up chromatically to *a* and back down. Examples:

Always strive for a light, relaxed, forward tone, which can be described to the children as "a happy, floating tone." The tone must never be forced, harsh or excessively loud.

b. Rhythm drills: imitating simple patterns clapped by the director, involving combinations of quarters, two eighths, four sixteenths, three triplet eighths, half notes and quarter rests, to be introduced in that sequence. Here are eight representative examples, each of which should be clapped separately by the director and responded to by clapping by the children.

c. Recognition of note values: identifying these notes from flash cards or blackboard, also finding them in printed music.

d. Singing of note values: establishing the quarter note as a beat, singing series of quarters, eighths, sixteenths and triplet eighths (as instructed by the director or as seen on flash cards or blackboard), while clapping or beating time. The syllable *ta* should be sung. Examples:

                        quarters
        sing: ta   ta   ta   ta
        clap: '   '   '   '

                        eighths
        ta   ta   ta   ta   ta   ta   ta   ta
         '   '   '   '

                        sixteenths
        tatatatatatatatatatatatatatatatata
         '   '   '   '

Eventually the half notes (two beats) and whole notes (four beats) should be added.

e. Learning and using the 3/4 and 4/4 conductor's patterns while singing rhythms similar to the above patterns in steps b and d.

3 pattern (3/4, 3/2, 3/8)   4 pattern (4/4, 4/2, 4/8)

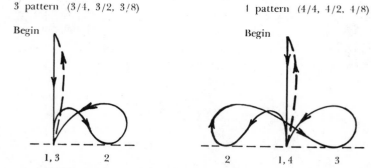

f. Recognition of intervals: identifying major scale steps and thirds when played on the piano, using the terms "step up," "step down," "skip up," and "skip down," and "stand" when the same note is repeated. Also finding these intervals on the piano keyboard.

g. Singing of intervals: singing these same intervals from given notes on the piano. Later reciting and singing them from music scores or from blackboard or flash cards.

h. Combination of rhythms and intervals: sight-reading simple musical scores involving rhythms similar to those studied, and intervals of steps and thirds. Conducting or beating time.

i. Unison singing: using songs involving rather short phrases and pitch ranges from middle *c* to octave *e* (ten notes). Using more complex intervals and rhythms, and employing florid, independent accompaniments.

j. Recognition and use of dynamics: using and identifying the terms forte, piano, mezzo piano and mezzo forte, also crescendo, decrescendo, ritardando and accelerando, while singing the vocalises in step a. Also employing the terms staccato and legato.

4. Repertoire. Music should be primarily hymns with texts easily understood by the children. But it can also include descants and solo parts from adult choir music, songs and anthems written especially for the age, simple spirituals and several "fun" songs such as those employing antiphonal responses and rounds.

5. Performances. This group should perform regularly, both alone and with other choirs.

Junior, Ages 9-11 or Grades 4-6

Rehearsal time: from 45 minutes to one hour.

1. Characteristics. Learning is accomplished faster by reading than by rote. Music potential is at an all-time high for children, although occasional pitch problems may still occur. Memorization powers are beginning to wane, therefore must be kept activated. Repetition is now important to stimulate memorization and retention. Disciplinary problems are increasing, but are usually the results of not having enough challenge or activity. Strict orders are quickly responded to, if accompanied by adult follow-through. Ambitions are even greater than their potential, therefore difficult assignments will be readily accepted if the end results look attractive. Yet simple tasks are often rejected. Activity must be fast-moving and with much variety. Group activities are well responded to, since this is an age for clubs and organizations. Many children are now taking piano or instrumental lessons and are being exposed to music training in school. Creativity is high, but will not be expressed freely unless encouraged. Boys' and girls' interests are beginning to differ widely, but they still work well together. In mixed groups, activities should be directed primarily to the boys. This approach is acceptable to the girls, but the opposite approach would be completely rejected by the boys.

2. Rehearsal goals. To teach precision in marching, standing and sitting; accuracy in details related to performance; immediate response to given orders. To develop good diction, intonation and a consciousness of good, relaxed vocal production. To teach more advanced music fundamentals and to apply them directly to sightsinging. To teach part singing. To encourage creative and performance skills in music. To build an appreciation for good music. To develop an understanding of worship and its implications. To teach hymnody, especially that which emphasizes the doctrines of salvation, man's responsibility to God and his dedication to service.

3. Rehearsal activities

a. Vocalization: using the exercises introduced in the primary choir, plus the following two:

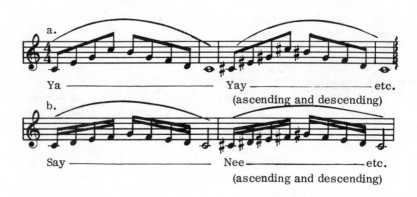

Ya ———————————————— Yay ——————— etc.

(ascending and descending)

Say ——————————— Nee ——————— etc.

(ascending and descending)

Continue to use the pure vowels *ah, ay, ee, oh* and *oo,* always preceding these with one of the following consonants:

s, y, n, to assure a forward placement of tone.

h, t, p, for precision of attacks.

Tones should continue to be light and relaxed, but range can be increased.

b. Study of breath support: inhaling and exhaling deep breaths with chest expanded and arms stretched upward until the breathing is felt to be expanding and contracting at the abdomen (just below the rib cage). Follow this with the singing of either long, sustained vowels or short panting sounds (such as "Ha, ha, ha") while observing the way in which the air gradually leaves the abdomen and is replaced underneath by a rising support from the diaphragm. Finally perform the same exercises with chest similarly expanded, but with arms down and shoulders relaxed.

c. Study of vocal production: comparing the extremely nasal (pinched) tone to the deep chest tone by having the children sing them both alternately on a single note, using the vowel *ah*. This will help them feel the two distinctly opposite characteristics of the human voice. Follow this with attempts to combine the two by beginning with a nasal tone and gradually moving the voice toward the chest until an even balance is felt.

d. Study of tonal contrasts: comparing tones which "spring" from one consonant to another with those which sustain vowel sounds for a longer duration. Exercises such as the following can be used:

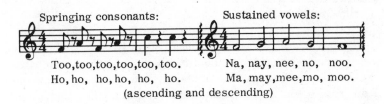

Springing consonants:

Too, too, too, too, too, too.
Ho, ho, ho, ho, ho, ho.

Sustained vowels:

Na, nay, nee, no, noo.
Ma, may, mee, mo, moo.

(ascending and descending)

These principles should then be applied to such songs as "Ding, Dong, Merrily on High" and "Deck the Halls with Boughs of Holly" (springing consonants), and "Fairest Lord Jesus" and "Were You There When They Crucified My Lord?" (sustained vowels), as well as songs which employ a combination of the two techniques, such as the familiar Easter song "Christ Arose" (stanza in sustained vowels and refrain in springing consonants). While this is an extreme approach to the techniques of crisp, bright tones and warm, legato sounds, it will help the child sense the contrasts between the two, and the approach can be modified when applying it to music.

e. Rhythm drills, note values and conducting: increasing the complexity of the rhythm combinations used in the primary choir and adding the following:

Dotted quarter and eighth notes:

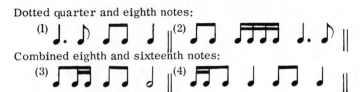

Combined eighth and sixteenth notes:

Conducting these exercises in 2/4, 3/4, 4/4 and 6/4 patterns.

2 pattern (2/4, 2/2, 2/8)   6 pattern (6/4, 6/8)

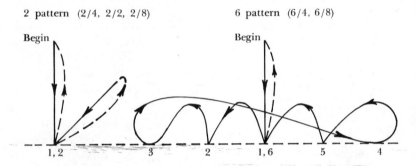

f. Interval drills: learning to hear, identify, sing and play (on the piano) the intervals of the 4ths, 5ths, and 6ths as built above and below the first note of a major scale, using the same procedures as found in rehearsal activities f and g for the primary choir.

g. Sightsinging: using syllables or numbers if desired, applying the principles of rhythm and interval studies to new music and exercises on the blackboard, while using the conductor's beat patterns.

h. Study of part singing: approaching it in six different ways:

(1) Building chords. Choir must be divided into three sections. All voices should begin on the same note and, while section one sustains the note, sections two and three should move to the next chord note. While section two sustains that note, three should move to the final chord note, resulting in a complete chord. Examples:

(2) Imitations (canons). Choir is divided into two or three sections. Section one begins by singing an exercise similar to the following:

The other sections enter at the asterisks (*) and keep singing in "round" fashion as illustrated:

(3) Singing in thirds or sixths. The choir is divided into two sections, each singing a third or a sixth apart on scale portions as illustrated:

(4) Singing in contrary motion. Section one sings up the scale while section two sings down, as follows:

(5) Singing two contrasting patterns simultaneously. Section one sings a five tone pattern while section two ascends or descends the scale as illustrated:

Other contrasting patterns, such as broken chords against scales, etc., should be attempted for interest and variety.

(6) Singing melodies with descants, such as found in some hymnals and in standard choral literature.

i. Unison and part singing: using longer phrases which demand the application of breathing principles; ranges no lower than *b* flat or higher than *f* (12 notes); larger form anthems; music involving alto parts, descants and canons.

j. Recognition of musical terms: learning to observe expression markings such as allegro, vivace, largo and lento; continuing to employ dynamic markings learned in primary choir.

k. Preparation of music workbooks: completing prescribed assignments of drawing clefs, staves, notes, scales, intervals, key signatures and time signatures, to be done during the week and handed in at rehearsal time.

l. Composition contests: occasionally permitting members to submit original poems or melodies to be judged by the director for awards or achievement points.

m. Hymn memorization: learning and memorizing at least one hymn per month, based on a prepared plan for the entire music department or in conjunction with the Christian education department.

4. Performances. Of all the children's choirs, the junior group is usually the most dependable in performances. It should be used frequently alone, as well as with the adult groups and other children's choirs. It should be given opportunities to sing in combined choir festivals with other choirs from neighboring churches. It should also sing occasionally at hospitals, rest homes, on caroling trips and many other places.

Junior High, Ages 12-14 or Grades 7-9

Rehearsal time: one hour.

1. Characteristics. Musical potential is largely dependent upon previous training or choir experience. Unless formerly nurtured and developed, memorization powers are very low. Resistance toward memorization is evident. Boys' and girls' interests are directly opposite. The boy prefers to be with other boys of his own age, but the girl, while also basically clannish, enjoys having the boys around. Both are physically awkward, but maturity is greater in the girl than in the boy. Singing gives the boy very little satisfaction, while the girl's voice is beginning to develop strength and maturity. Musical interests will center around instruments for the boys, but the girls may be interested in studying voice. However, neither will want to perform in public unless they are with a large group. Interests change rapidly and unpredictably, alternating from childlike interests to adult thoughts.

2. Rehearsal goals

For the boys: to stimulate interest in other aspects of music at a time when singing is no longer pleasurable. To prevent anything that will inadvertently harm the changing voice, such as attempts to sing bass before the voice has fully settled. To provide a link between that which has been done in previous choirs and that which will be resumed in the high school group.

For the girls: to continue working on the fundamentals of voice production begun in the junior choir. To develop greater ability in two- and three-part singing. To expand vocal ranges and to begin determining voice placements (sopranos, altos, mezzo sopranos).

For both: to teach more advanced music fundamentals. To develop an acquaintance with master composers and great compositions. To nurture creativity and encourage serious study of instruments or voice. To preserve memorization powers. To teach hymns and anthems which present the basic doctrines of the church.

3. *Rehearsal activities*

a. Vocalization: singing vocalises used by junior choir. For the boys, not much emphasis, keeping the ranges from about *f* to *f* (surrounding middle *c*). For the girls, a gradual increase in high and low ranges, working on evenness of quality as the ranges increase; increased emphasis on breath support and tonal contrasts.

b. Sightsinging: increasing the difficulty of melodies to be read at sight; increasing intervals to the 7ths, 9ths and 10ths.

c. Part singing: For the boys, the learning of tenor or cambiata parts to music sung with the girls. For the girls, an increase in the use of three-part music written for treble trios or choruses (S. S. A.).

d. Instrumental study: working with instruments, studying the principles of each, allowing members to demonstrate on their own instruments. This is especially good activity for the boys.

e. Music appreciation: studying the lives of composers, their works, their styles, using recordings, assigning book reports, or probably following a prescribed study of music literature.

f. Preparation of workbooks: following the sequence begun in the junior choir.

g. Study and memorization of hymns: learning at least one hymn a month, but also learning the background of the hymns and the lives of the composers and authors.

4. Repertoire. Music should include standard hymns and anthems, plus gospel songs with very strong texts and music. Music should include much unison material, plus three-part (soprano, alto, cambiata or tenor) music.

5. *Performances.* Performances will depend on the ability and size of the group. If an embarrassing experience, performance should be limited. On the other hand, this could be one of the best-sounding groups in the graded choir program.

High School, Ages 15-17 or Grades 10-12

Rehearsal time: one hour or more.

1. *Characteristics.* Music potential is again dependent upon background. If the school system and the church choirs have provided a boy with several years of choir and band experience, he can be an excellent contribution to the choir. Boys' voices, though not fully mature, have usually settled. Girls' voices will be gaining

strength, but will frequently become colorless and piercing, partly due to the fact that the girls are trying to increase their volume. Learning is accomplished in adult ways, as youth possess adult capabilities. Memorization powers are increasing now, due to the demands made upon them in high school study. Repetition will not be well accepted unless there are obvious purposes for it. It is often misinterpreted to be a hindrance to progress.

Attitudes toward adult leadership vary rapidly. Often the youth will desire the advice of an adult, but will consider the advice to be jeopardizing to his individuality, or to be based on outmoded ideas. He wants to be challenged, but often feels that too much is expected of him. He is "duty-minded" and accepts responsibilities and positions seriously. He has a strong desire to conquer difficult things, but sometimes recants if they demand too much "thinking." He responds best in mixed groups, is socially minded, and considers every activity a potential social affair.

2. Rehearsal goals. To teach greater insight into music, its structure, background and message. To develop the ability to think and hear good tone, blend and interpretation. To promote self-organization within the choir and to teach responsibility. To prepare some for future careers in music, others for full-time service for Christ. To develop learning habits. To build a substantial repertoire of hymns, anthems and larger choral works. To encourage growth in appreciation for music and other arts. To develop spiritual leadership and increased awareness of the potentials in the ministry of music.

3. Rehearsal activities

a. Vocalization: continuing with vocal exercises similar to those begun in the junior choir, but with increased emphasis on building range. The vowel *ah* should be the one most frequently used, but occasionally the *ay* vowel should be used for the boys, and the *ee* vowel for the girls, especially when brightness is needed. The darker vowels, *oh* and *oo,* should seldom be used, and only after the others have been practiced. The soft consonants *y, s* and *n* should still precede all vowels.

b. Breath support, voice production and tonal contrasts: as studied previously, but more carefully applied to singing.

c. Blend: singing chords with a series of very slowly changing vowels as indicated:

Up and down chromatically, seek to "tune" each chord until the blend is the best possible, training the singers' ears to hear the resultant effects of: (1) perfectly pitched tones, (2) balanced parts, (3) well-shaped vowels, (4) well-supported tones and (5) free, effortless tonal production. These chords should be practiced in many variances of loudness, contrasts and degrees of speed. The vocal results should be a combination of:

A relaxed jaw and free singing area (mouth and throat)

The feeling of effortless production

Tones that are forwardly placed

Vowels that are pure.

d. Music appreciation: conducting discussions, assigning research projects on composers, major oratorios, symphonies or related subjects, listening to recordings and attending symphony concerts as a social affair.

e. Hymn memorization: continuing the hymn-of-the-month plan, using hymns of deeper meaning, plus gospel songs of personal challenge or dedication.

f. Development of ensembles: organizing and training quartets, trios and other vocal and instrumental combinations.

g. Encouraging of individual talents: incorporating talented youths into the church program as vocal soloists (if qualified), accompanists, and leaders of small ensembles, part rehearsals and congregational or departmental singing.

4. *Repertoire.* Except when it is necessary to use smaller voicings, such as soprano, alto and baritone music, the repertoire of the high school group should hardly differ from adult choir music.

5. *Performances.* This group should perform regularly, perhaps even replacing the adult choir on certain occasions. It should com-

bine with the adult choir for festival numbers or in the presentation of cantatas and oratorios.

General Rehearsal Procedures

The director should outline the materials he wishes to cover in each rehearsal. His plan for the rehearsal should be well thought out, but should not follow the same pattern every week. Variety is an excellent stimulus to interest and enthusiasm. The following should serve as a guide to preparing the weekly rehearsal sessions:

1. Opening prayer or prayer hymn and devotional thought.
2. Vocalization drills.
3. Review of music previously learned, with special emphasis on selections which will be sung at the next appearance.
4. Other drills listed in rehearsal activities.
5. Study of new music.
6. More drills.
7. Review of the hymn-of-the-month.
8. Discussion of projects or workbooks and necessary announcements.
9. More drills.
10. Reserve for whatever review is most necessary (3, 5 or 7).
11. Closing prayer.

There are many conditions which would necessitate major changes in the rehearsal procedures. They include:

a. The weather. More vocal work is sometimes necessary when the weather is cold and windy. On the other hand, it is better to limit the vocal demands when inclement weather has affected the throats and nasal passages.

A sudden change of weather, such as on the first real day of spring, greatly diminishes the attention span of both old and young, often causing additional discipline problems. On such a day, more emphasis should be placed on variety in the rehearsal, and the more active drills should replace those which demand too much concentration.

b. Pressures of performances. At certain times, nearly all drills (except vocalizing) must be omitted because of the pressures of preparing new music or larger works. Although this will happen frequently, it should never become a common procedure, as it will then reflect on the director's inability to plan ahead.

c. Poor attendance. It is impractical to introduce new material when a rehearsal is not well attended, as it will necessitate too much repetition when the absentees return. It is also quite unrewarding to attempt good blend at such a time. Review work and drills should then be emphasized.

Choir Robes and Vestments

According to I Chronicles 15:27, David and all his singers were robed for the great festive occasion of bringing the ark into Jerusalem.

When taking part in a service of worship, it is important that all choir members be uniformly dressed so that attention will not be focused upon the individual, but rather upon the message which the choir is presenting through song. The most common choir apparel is the choir robe; however, other type uniforms may also be used.

Robes or other vestments should not be prohibitive in cost to most churches, since they can be easily prepared by parents of the choir members or by a churchwomen's society. The atmosphere which robes contribute to the services will more than compensate for the work involved. Not only this, but they will have an arresting effect upon the children who wear them, giving them a greater sense of belonging, and also serving as an inducement to better behavior.

Recreational and Social Activities

Social activities are essential to all choral groups, but their importance intensifies as the child grows older. It is advisable that the minister of music plan a yearly program of recreational activities designed to meet the needs of each group. The details of these events should be handled by the choir sponsors and officers, and should include simple refreshments before or after rehearsals when the schedule permits, tours of museums, radio or television studios and other places of interest, plus attendance at concerts or special musical functions.

SUGGESTED REHEARSAL MATERIALS

HARRISON, L. A. and McKINNEY, B. B. *Practical Music Lessons* (Parts 1 and 2). Nashville: Broadman Press, 1950.
A study of the fundamentals of music.

OLVERA, J. *The Ups and Downs of Music.* Park Ridge, Ill.: Neil A. Kjos Music Co., 1959.
Songs and exercises designed to teach pitch and intervals.

Scarmolin, A. L. *The Chorister's Daily Dozen*. New York: Pro Art Publications, 1951.

Exercises designed for developing beautiful tone, proper breathing and clarity of diction.

Tkach, P. *Vocal Technic*. Park Ridge, Ill.: Neil A. Kjos Music Co., 1948.

Instructions and accompanying exercises for developing correct voice production and the fundamentals of sightsinging.

RECOMMENDED READING

Holcomb, C. A. *Methods and Materials for Graded Choirs*. Nashville: Broadman Press, 1948.

Howard, F. E. *The Child-Voice in Singing*. London: Novello and Co., 1909.

Lovelace, A. C. and Rice, W. C. *Music and Worship in the Church*. Nashville: Abingdon Press, 1960.

McKenzie, Duncan. *Training the Boy's Changing Voice*. New Brunswick: Rutgers University Press, 1956.

Urang, G. *Church Music—For the Glory of God*. Moline, Ill.: Christian Service Foundation, 1956.

Chapter 13

THE ADULT CHOIR

Most Christian churches in America maintain either an adult choir of mixed voices or a men's and boys' choir as the ministering musical group in the worship service. The all-male groups are usually found where the European traditions in liturgical worship are observed, while mixed choirs are used in both liturgical and nonliturgical churches.

Background and Development of Church Choirs

1. Old Testament: men's choirs. Only adult men, aged thirty and over, were used for Old Testament worship. Women are recorded as singing only informally in ceremonies outside of the temple. Miriam and the other women sang a song of triumph when the children of Israel succeeded in crossing the Red Sea (Exodus 15:20,21). When David returned as victor over the Philistine giant, the women responded with a song of victory, using "instruments of musick" (I Sam. 18:6,7). Ecclesiastes refers to using men and women singers, but again in an informal way.

2. Early church: men and boys. The tradition of using men and boys probably did not begin until the fourth century, when choir schools were established to train the choristers. This continued to be the only type of choir used in the Christian church until the eighteenth century. For some years during that period, instrumental music was considered unfit for worship. Consequently, the choir made the only musical contribution to Christian worship for centuries. Finally, in the thirteenth century, instruments were reintroduced into the churches by popular demand in some countries.

3. Eighteenth century: mixed voices. Although the use of adult mixed choirs is often considered an American-born tradition, the practice began in Germany in the eighteenth century. The simplified order of worship used, plus the emphasis placed upon congregational involvement in the services, led to the popular use

154

of nonprofessional choirs, in which both men and women were encouraged to participate without choir school training.

America, on the other hand, suffered an "aversion toward musical culture that is without parallel in history,"[1] brought upon her by the Pilgrim settlers. Until the middle of the eighteenth century, only a few traditional tunes were sung from memory, and the use of choirs or printed music was forbidden in the church.

One group which took exception to this was the Trinity Anglican Church in New York. In 1693, it imported singers and organists from England, probably forming the first church choir in America.

The first choir of mixed voices in America was the Sacred Singing School, founded in Stoughton, Massachusetts, in 1774, by William Billings. Its membership of forty-eight included thirty-one women. Although this was the first stable organization of amateur singers in America, the quality of its work was not good, and it was soon surpassed in excellence by the Handel and Haydn Society, organized in Boston in 1815.

The first oratorio performance in America was given on Christmas of that year, when the society, using ninety men and ten women singers, performed the first part of Haydn's *Creation* and several small works by Handel. In 1818, the same group presented the first American performance of Handel's *Messiah*. It was not until 1827, when Dr. Lowell Mason became president of the society, that the distribution of men's and women's voices was equalized. Not long after that, the churches began to use adult mixed choirs.

The Effectiveness of Adult Choirs

In comparing adult church choirs to traditional men's and boys' choirs, Archibald Davison claims that the adult choir is "by far the most effective choral organization."[2] Considering the choir as a ministering agent to worship, this cannot help but be true. There are at least two good reasons for this.

1. The trends in musical education have changed. Today our churches often have more capable women singers than men, and would be destitute of talent if the women were not used. This would not have been the case in the nineteenth century, as women were rarely given an opportunity to study music. When the Sacred Harmonic Society was organized in 1832 in London, women sing-

---

[1] *Encyclopaedia Britannica*, 1959, V, 620.
[2] A. T. Davison, *Protestant Church Music in America* (Boston: E. C. Schirmer Music Company, 1933), p. 167.

ers had to be imported from northern and midland counties because of the scarcity of trained voices in London.

2. Maturity is essential to performing an effective ministry. The effectiveness of the ministry of children's choirs, or those involving children, is limited in part to the ability of the children to comprehend spiritual things. This does not imply there can be no ministry in such groups; in fact, it is quite the contrary. Yet the ministry is of a different nature, as it takes a well-developed attitude and outlook on the potential of sacred music, plus a comprehension of the message it contains, to capably and effectively lead a congregation in worship every Sunday morning. In short, one must be able to "sing with the spirit and with the understanding also" (I Cor. 14:15).

The Use of Volunteers

Both Davison and Lorenz advocate the use of volunteer choirs rather than professional singers. Lorenz states, "Twenty voices of moderate range and melodiousness can do more to lift the spirit of the worshipper than the best trained quartet in the land."[3]

The practice of engaging professional voices is certainly permissible and sometimes necessary, but the choir itself should be open to the laity. The utilization of church members not only draws the choir and congregation closer together but also provides an avenue of Christian service for those who participate. This does not infer that qualifications are not necessary for choir membership. On the contrary, the person who desires to serve God in this way must meet the demands of the stewardship which has been entrusted to him.

Qualifications for Membership

In order that the choir may have the most possible effectiveness, the following requirements should be considered:

1. Age. Concerning the most effective age, many authorities continue to hold to the Levitical practice of employing those between the ages of thirty and fifty. At these ages, vocal ability and spiritual maturity have usually reached their highest peak of attainment. Age limit will, however, be largely determined by the amount of talent available, and will frequently include younger adults and often teen-agers. The wider age span is highly desirable if it results in a more adequate size and a better balance of voices.

[3] E. S. Lorenz, *Practical Church Music* (New York: Fleming H. Revell Co., 1909), p. 250.

In other instances it would be better to be more restrictive in age requirements so as to prevent an oversized group. In summary, it is not necessary to set any particular restrictions in age unless it is for the betterment of the choir.

2. Moral and spiritual life. Without exception, all adult choir members should agree to maintain the highest moral and spiritual standards possible. There are, however, varied schools of thought as to whether or not participation in choirs should be restricted to born-again believers in Christ, or even to those who are members of the church. One factor to consider is that an unconverted person may be brought to Christ through his active association with the choir, thereby making the choir an evangelistic effort within its own organization. On the other hand, the unsaved person could become a hindrance to the choir if he refused to maintain high moral principles and Christian conduct. Therefore, the question concerning membership and conversion experience must be decided according to the individual situation, but the standards of living must be enforced without reservation.

3. Attendance. A choir is not well trained unless its rehearsals are well attended. Normally, all members should be required to attend all rehearsals and services unless unavoidably detained, at which time they should notify the secretary or director. The member who fails in these obligations should be removed from the membership, but certain conditions should be provided which would permit him to be reinstated. Sometimes exceptions must be made in communities where most of the members work in alternating shifts and must miss frequent services and rehearsals as a result, or when a person's work requires a certain amount of travel. Despite the many modifications that will have to be made to adjust to local and personal situations, every member should be required to maintain the most regular attendance possible.

4. Musical qualifications. Obviously, a church which is blessed with higher than average musical ability can be very selective, but it is also possible for other choirs less endowed to maintain basic minimal musical requirements to be met by all members. The three areas of musical evaluation should be:

a. Vocal ability. Not every good choir member will be a potential soloist, but he should have a pleasing tone quality, be able to sing on pitch, and should possess no outstanding vocal defects that would prove an impediment to good blend.

b. Musicianship. Although reading ability can be quickly developed through constant practice, the inability to hear pitches and to sense rhythms is usually more difficult to correct.

c. Willingness to learn. Most vocal and musical problems can be overcome when there is willingness and a large portion of optimism to go with it. As Lorenz puts it, "Some of these 'ugly ducklings' have a very strange way of turning out to be swans under the educational advantages work in the choir affords."[4] The person who is fearful of new ventures, or who lacks confidence and initiative, is a greater risk than the one who accepts challenges willingly and energetically even if he has poor musical ability.

5. Interest in the ministry. No person should become a member of a church choir unless he has an interest in serving the Lord. He should think of choir work as a ministry, "not as pleasing men, but God" (I Thess. 2:4). Coupled with this should be an ardent love for music and a compassion for others. This threefold interest cannot help but strengthen the spiritual impact of the choir as it endeavors to reach men and women for God through the medium of music.

6. A declaration of dedication. Before a new choir member is accepted, he should be given an interview and an audition, unless abilities and other qualifications have already been made evident. When specific areas of weakness are made apparent through the audition, he should promise to try to correct them. He should be given a membership card to sign, on which he agrees to uphold the standards of the choir and be regular and attentive to his responsibilities. He should also be given a copy of the choir constitution, which would contain the above requirements, a brief outline of the ministries of the choir (to be discussed next) and the organizational structure of the group.

Ministries of the Adult Choir

The adult choir ministers primarily to the congregation and only secondarily to itself. This constitutes one of the greatest differences between the ministries of the adult and children's choirs. The most important functions of the children's groups are providing training for spiritual and musical growth for their members, and secondarily, giving opportunities for Christian service. Although the adult choir also provides these two things for its members, first consideration will be given to its ministry to the person in the pew.

1. Ministry in worship. There are three biblically ordained as-

[4] op. cit., p. 254.

pects of the choir's ministry in worship: to lead, to represent and to instruct.

a. To lead in worship. In Old Testament times, the choir took the leadership in worship, and its singing was usually followed by a response from the congregation, sometimes in an act of worship (II Chron. 29:28), other times in rejoicing (23:13), or even in shouting the praises of God (Ezra 3:11).

In like manner, the church choir is in a position of natural leadership today, as it participates from Sunday to Sunday in the worship services. This is true for the following three reasons:

In the first place, the choir is usually located in a place where it can be observed by all or most of the congregation, and is therefore looked to for guidance during the services.

Second, the well-prepared choir has taken time to rehearse the service. It has not only reviewed the regular parts of worship but has also been informed ahead of time concerning any innovations in the order. It has drilled in rising and sitting as a unit and is also prepared to lead forth in the responsive readings, hymns, litanies and other parts of the service in which the congregation is expected to participate.

Finally, as a result, the members of the choir are in better position to understand and thereby respond to the spirit of the service. Through rehearsing, they should be able to see how each portion of the service contributes to the overall worship experience desired, and should be conscious of the specific theme or emphasis which is to be followed throughout the hour. If these things are meaningful to them personally, they will be able to convey the spirit of the entire service to the congregation through their attitudes and actions.

b. To represent the congregation before God. Another task of the Levitical choirs was to "minister before the ark of the Lord, and to record, and to thank and praise the Lord God of Israel" (I Chron. 16:4). By singing anthems and responses which are directed to God in supplication, today's church choirs perform the priestly function of representing the people before God.

c. To instruct the congregation. The Apostle Paul advocates the use of music as a tool of spiritual instruction: "Teaching and admonishing one another in psalms and hymns and spiritual songs" (Col. 3:16). The choir anthem is often used to interpret the Word of God and to teach the doctrines relating to Christian experience.

2. *Ministry to the choir member.* The ingoing ministry of the choir member is fourfold:

a. It is spiritual, in that it gives him constant opportunities to peruse the Word of God and the doctrines of Christianity through the texts which he rehearses and performs.

b. It is educational, in that he is given training in self-expression, music and the disciplines of learning.

c. It is serviceable, in that it provides him with chances to use his talents to honor the Lord.

d. It is social, in that it offers him Christian fellowship. The ministry of Christian fellowship is given to him in the choir rehearsal itself, as well as in social functions, choir retreats and special outings. The social ministry is a vital part of the functions of the choir, especially to those who may otherwise be deprived of such fellowship in their daily employment or family life. In addition to the fellowship aspect, the above social activities accomplish other purposes as well.

(1) They develop greater unity within the group. Good choral singing is dependent upon unanimity of thought and purpose. Social functions help to break down any barriers that would tend to hinder this.

(2) They help cultivate new insights into the ministry. It has already been established that the choir may include a few persons who have not yet surrendered their lives to the Lord. As a consequence, they cannot fully comprehend the extent of the ministry in which they are involved, nor can they fulfill all the personal obligations which befall the Christian choir member. Social functions can help them become aware of their need and can be the means of drawing these folk to the place of commitment. With this in mind, the activities should include times of personal testimony by other choir members, inspirational speakers and other forms of challenge. These will be a ministry not only to those mentioned but also to the entire membership. Loyalty can be encouraged by honoring those who have been faithful in attendance for the season.

3. *Ministry to the community.* Both the church and the community look to the choir to help establish cultural levels. The church is judged by the kind of music used in the services, as well as the level of its performance. What the choir sings reflects upon the educational background of the membership, its tastes and its social refinements.

The newcomer to the community will use the music as a partial guide in determining whether or not he will feel at home among the people of the church, should he choose to worship there regularly. The unchurched person who attends a service or musical program will judge the spiritual depth and sincerity of the people by the texts and music used and the attitude expressed in singing.

In these ways, the ministry of the church and its effectiveness and influences upon the community are largely dependent upon the choir.

Another medium of influence on the community is the cooperation shown in civic activities and community functions. The choir can be a witness to the community by singing at worthy functions which do not demand the lowering of spiritual standards and do not interfere with regular church activities, such as dedications of civic institutions (hospitals, schools), interchurch campaigns and community benefits. Occasional visits to local rest homes and other institutions to conduct brief concerts will prove to the community that the church is interested in the welfare of others.

4. *The choir member's own ministry.* The ministry of the choir member extends much farther than the ministry of the choir itself. Whereas he is just a part of a ministering group while in the worship service, he is an individual witness as soon as he leaves the choir loft. His association with the choir makes this so. There are at least three ways in which he shows the extent of his discipleship both to the church members and the community.

a. By his own personal conduct. His moral standards, ethical and business principles, personal habits and social involvements all bespeak his testimony for Christ.

b. By his attitude toward the church. A choir member must also be a loyal attendant at the functions of the church, an ardent supporter of its activities and a prayerful backer of its spiritual endeavors.

c. By his attitude toward his choir responsibility. This is evidenced by good attendance, promptness, cooperation, support and respect for those with whom he labors in the work.

Because of his weekly participation in the public service, the choir member is probably the most conspicuous lay worker in the church. Consequently, he becomes a symbol of what a Christian worker should be. It is important that he represent true discipleship "in word, in conversation, in charity, in spirit, in faith, in purity" (I Tim. 4:12).

Adult Choir Organization

1. Officers and committees. Active officers and committees are an asset to the choir, an aid to the director, an incentive to the choir members and an assurance of a more successful ministry. Unfortunately, many choirs elect them without giving them specific directives, or choose them on the basis of popularity rather than qualifications. As a result, extra work is thrust upon the director, or many important operative functions are neglected. The duties of each officer, as indicated in a preceding chapter, should be included in a choir constitution, which should be presented to all members upon becoming a part of the group.

2. The constitution. Contents of the constitution should include:

a. Name of the organization and general objectives, based on the ministries of the choir discussed herein.

b. General organization, including the minister of music, the accompanists, the music committee and its relationship to the choir program.

c. Qualifications for membership, as stated herein and adapted to the particular needs of the choir, with a specific statement whether an audition must be given and a statement of purpose must be signed.

d. Officers and duties, frequency and time of elections.

e. Committees and their responsibilities.

f. Rules and regulations for members, stating rehearsal times and service responsibilities, attendance requirements and penalties, times of business meetings, socials and other functions.

A special committee, consisting of several officers and members, representatives from the music committee and the director, should be delegated to compose the constitution. Upon its completion, it should be submitted to the choir, the music committee and then the church board for final approval.

The Choir Rehearsal

The effectiveness of a church choir depends largely on its rehearsal. Good choral singing is not obtained without months—even years—of consistent work on building voices, developing musicianship, learning notes, perfecting pieces and enlarging concepts of the ministry of music. The rehearsal is the place where this must be done.

1. Rehearsal time. Time of the rehearsal should be on a regular basis on a designated night each week. It should be no less than one hour and no more than two, the ideal length being about one and one-half hours. The church schedule should be so arranged that no other activities will conflict with this appointed time, except for an annual churchwide evangelistic or missionary series. During these special efforts, provision should be made for shortened rehearsals, unless the responsibilities of the choir are not continued during that time.

Choir members should agree to arrange all their personal activities so that they will not conflict with rehearsals and performances. At best, there are far too many unavoidable circumstances, such as sickness, work responsibilities and family obligations, which reduce regularity in rehearsal attendance.

2. *Rehearsal techniques.* Although there are many ways to conduct a choir rehearsal, the following points will help the director in his effort to get maximum results in a limited time:

a. More singing, less talking. A brief explanation, followed by an immediate application to the music, is far more successful than the lecture approach. When less is verbalized, the choir develops a greater aptitude for responding to the conductor's beat, bodily gestures and facial expressions. Constant activity also tends to lessen the private conversations which often take place during a rehearsal.

b. Repetition with purpose. Repetition is an effective tool of learning, but not unless attention is focused upon desired accomplishments through repetition. It is unwise to simply "sing it again" without suggesting that the singers concentrate on improving the diction, breathing, expression, or on watching out for difficult intervals or rhythms.

c. Avoid part rehearsals except when absolutely necessary. Most difficult passages can be conquered by slow, deliberate practice of all voices together. This gives the singers time to hear and find their notes, while at the same time associating them with the rest of the harmony. If this approach is not successful, the individual problems should be sung in unison by the entire choir, rather than by the individual voices or sections. This gives them the added assistance of all the better sight readers in the choir, gives the entire choir some valuable sight-reading experience and eliminates idleness in other sections of the choir.

d. Use sectional rehearsals for larger problems. If the harmonies are complex and hard to hear, or if contrapuntal music is being learned, each vocal section should go to a separate room for a designated time of part rehearsing. Sectional leaders who can play the piano should be selected. If such persons are not available, double part rehearsals could be held instead, with the director and the accompanist each taking two sections at a time. Division of parts will depend on the music. Usually it is best to rehearse the two women's parts and the two men's parts in separate sections. However, in some of the contrapuntal works of Haydn, Beethoven, Handel, Mendelssohn and others, similar themes and other devices are employed for the soprano and tenor, and contrasting parts for the alto and bass; therefore it would be practical to rehearse them in this way. Immediately following the sectional rehearsals the entire choir should sing together the piece which has been studied.

e. Analyze the problem sources. All problems in choral singing can be categorized as either learning, production or performance.

(1) Learning problems. No portion of music is so complex that its learning difficulties cannot be traced to one of the following: rhythm, interval, harmony or pitch. If the *rhythm* cannot be felt, it should be recited rhythmically on a monotone until learned. If the *intervals* are hard to find, they should be analyzed as to their size (4th, 5th, etc.) and drilled on individually. Any possible association of the interval with familiar sounds (e.g., a major 6th sounds like the first interval in the refrain of "He Lives," or the beginning of "My Bonnie Lies over the Ocean") will hasten the learning process. If certain *harmonic sounds* or *pitches* are hard to hear, the entire choir should "lead into them" and sustain them while the accompanist seeks to correct the errors, thus giving the ear opportunity to get accustomed to the new sounds.

(2) Production problems. The problems in production can be traced to one of the following: breath support, tone quality, intonation, diction and balance of voices. The director must train himself to discern between all of these, and should treat them individually when they occur. This can be done by sustaining the chord in question, while seeking to get the desired results. Drill exercises, similar to those found in graded choir rehearsal suggestions, will help to eliminate many of these problems, and will train the choir members to become aware of the techniques necessary for good vocal production.

(3) Performance problems. Assuming that the learning and production problems are well under control, the remaining problems can be traced to attacks, releases, phrasing, blend, tempi, contrasts, quick changes or dynamics. Attacks and releases are often closely related to rhythms and consonants, and can sometimes be con-

quered simultaneously. Good phrasing is dependent upon breath control; blend is practically unobtainable without good production, or at least a consistency of tone and diction; the problems of tempi, contrasts, quick changes and dynamics must be approached individually.

f. Concentrate on small portions at a time. It is a time-consuming habit to always rehearse an anthem from the beginning to the end, especially when the major difficulties are usually in two or three specific places throughout the composition. The most successful way of rehearsing is that of drilling on these small segments, whether they consist of three notes or three measures, until the problems are solved. Considering the fact that such a short passage can be repeated several times in a few minutes, the accomplishments will more than repay for the time and effort.

g. Practice without accompaniment. Choir members often tend to depend upon the accompanist to establish pitches, rhythms and tempi. It has been proved, however, that the choir which rehearses unaccompanied much of the time develops better musicianship among its ranks. A worthy goal is to be able to sing all anthems without accompaniment before using them in the church service—even those which demand accompaniment for performance. Even if the choir does not reach the level of a good-sounding *a cappella* choir, it will improve rapidly in pitch, breath support and intonation, and the choir members will learn to respond to the conductor's direction.

h. Approach musical interpretation by way of the textual contents. Expression will be gained much faster if phrases are referred to as "majestic, victorious, dominating or exuberant" rather than merely "loud." These descriptive words carry more meaning and also adapt themselves to the textual contents of an anthem of praise. The amateur choir member will understand the reason for the dynamics needed, therefore will respond more enthusiastically to both music and message. As an example of interpretive suggestions, consider the hymn "Spirit of God, Descend upon My Heart." The tempo and dynamic of the beginning would be simply "slow and soft," which would result in an inadequate performance. However, if it is sung with the "intensity and fervor of a devout believer in Christ who realizes his own inadequacies and his desperate need for the Holy Spirit to control his life," it will doubtless result in a greater communication of thought. Perhaps this is what Paul meant when he suggested that we "sing with the spirit, and with the understanding also" (I Cor. 14:15).

i. Establish definite goals. It is too easy to allow a choir rehearsal to become little more than a rehearsal of notes and a preparation of anthems for performance. In order to counteract this nonprogressive spirit, it is necessary to establish specific goals which are both desirable and within reach of the choir. Periodic emphases should be placed upon the perfecting of each of the important aspects of good singing, possibly beginning with diction and later turning toward good attacks, breath support or phrasing. During each emphasis, choir members should be made aware of the goals they are expected to reach and reminded of them frequently. Members and director alike will delight in seeing goals reached from week to week, therefore will be more optimistic when faced with new challenges. The genius of such an approach is to know how demanding each goal can be without discouraging the weaker members.

j. Be ever complimentary, always optimistic, yet never content. Two of the dangers in choir work are: becoming so complimentary that the choir becomes complacent, and being so discontent that the choir becomes resentful or discouraged. It is hard to find a balance between the two extremes, especially when the degree of talent varies greatly among the members. The wise director will be complimentary when even the smallest attainments are reached, but will always follow each compliment with a new, fresh challenge, and at the same time will show confidence in their ability to progress even further than they have.

3. *Suggested rehearsal procedure.* The contents of a rehearsal are determined by the desired achievements. For this reason, it is impossible to suggest a plan that will be useful in every situation. It is suggested that rehearsals be planned carefully each week, but with enough flexibility to allow for unexpected problems which might occur during the session.

The following is a general outline which will serve as a guide in planning the rehearsal.

a. Opening prayer or brief devotions.

b. Vocalization, using selected vocalises for warm-up and development. .

c. Rehearsal of anthems for next appearance. After this is done, the director should be able to determine how much time must be devoted to immediate needs, and thus adapt the remaining time schedule accordingly.

d. Rehearsal of music to be used for the following three or four weeks, in the order of its usage.

e. Five-minute break for announcements or for relaxation.

f. Review of the morning worship service, singing hymns and responses, briefly discussing the general theme of the service, if any.

g. Introduction of new material, or work on cantata, oratorio or other future musical program.

h. Return to the anthems to be sung in next appearance, with special drill on difficult sections. Possibly it would be wise to move to the choir loft for the remainder of the rehearsal.

i. Closing remarks by the director concerning the specific challenges facing the choir in the near or immediate future, plus a recapitulation of the musical goals he desires to see achieved.

j. Closing prayer.

The average anthem should never be practiced for more than a half hour at a time. When particular problems occur in steps c and f, it is advisable to return to these for three or more brief reviews throughout the rehearsal. The three or more concentrated drills will accomplish more than an extended period.

The Choir Music

Joseph Ashton refers to choir music as the "highest form of church music." He continues by stating that it is "something more than a thing of musical beauty and interest; its function is religious."[5]

This statement suggests the complexity of the problem facing the conductor when he selects music for his choir, for it must be both musically attractive and spiritually functional. The task of finding such music is not an easy one, and it is made even more difficult by the large number of anthems being published. One must not only be able to separate the good from the bad—a formidable task in itself—but also be able to select from the good that which would be practical for his own use. Much has already been said concerning the choice of texts. Here are some things which must be considered in choosing music:

1. *Consider the needs of the choir.* The needs of each choir vary according to the following physical characteristics:

a. Size of choir. Anthems intended for large festival choirs, or those with multiple parts, will seldom fulfill the needs of the small choir. It is not sufficient to be able to sing the parts required. The choir must also be able to produce the fullness of sound needed in such an anthem.

b. Balance of parts. Many volunteer choirs suffer from a lack

[5] J. N. Ashton, *Music in Worship* (Boston: Pilgrim Press, 1943), p. 122.

of equal voicing in each section. Most contrapuntal music and anthems with divided parts will expose these weaknesses. Anthems with limited voicing, such as three-part music (soprano, alto and baritone), will compensate for this lack. If there are enough voices to maintain the four parts, although not equally distributed, four-part anthems which are basically harmonic should be used.

c. Voice range limitations. Most untrained voices will sound acceptable in moderate ranges, but are ineffective on extreme high and low notes. Music should be chosen on the basis of the best ranges of each section.

d. Solo voices available. Normally an anthem requiring a solo voice which is not available should be rejected; however, at times it is possible to make substitutions which will result in a very effective performance. Suggested substitutions are alto for baritone or bass, soprano for tenor, an entire section instead of one voice, a youth or children's choir singing the solo part, or the entire choir singing in unison.

e. Reading ability and musicianship. Both the length and the difficulty of the music selected should be determined by the number of good sight readers available. It is wise to estimate the time that will be needed to learn the music. If the time is within reason and the music seems to be worth the effort that will need to be taken to learn it, the choice will probably be a good one.

f. Background and appreciation. The style of music used will be determined in part by that which has been used and accepted by the choir and congregation in the past. This does not suggest, however, that the director must cater to the present level of music appreciation, but it shows him where he must begin in his long-range plan of widening the expanse of musical acceptance.

g. Accompanists and their instruments. Choral repertoire contains many appropriate anthems of very little difficulty vocally, and enhanced by colorful and attractive accompaniments. These will be welcome additions to the choir library, if the organist or pianist is able to do better than average music, and if he has a good instrument on which to play.

2. *Consider the music itself.* A well-stocked choir library will include anthems of varied styles and texts. In building the choir repertoire for the year, the following factors should be observed:

a. The periods. For the sake of simplification, we will classify all music into five historical periods:

Early period—Bach, Handel, Byrd, Buxtehude, Purcell, Schutz and others

Classic period—Beethoven, Haydn and Mozart

Nineteenth Century—Mendelssohn, Grieg, Stainer, Dubois and others

Mild contemporary—Shaw, Thiman, Titcomb, McKay Williams, Clokey, Sateren, Mueller and others

Contemporary—Sowerby, Britten, Vaughan Williams and others.

The choir should select its music almost equally from the first four periods. Contemporary compositions may have to be used sparingly until a general acceptance has been gained. Sometimes it is even better to eliminate this period entirely until the mild contemporary has become more readily acceptable. Although the desire should always be to lead the choir and congregation into new musical experiences, one must know just how far he can go before he jeopardizes his ministry or loses contact with his people. That is why an equal balance is recommended.

b. Part distribution and form. The choir should use an assortment of unison anthems, *a cappella* settings, chorales, hymn anthems, contrapuntal works, plus anthems built around solos, those with predominant accompaniments, and those built on pure harmonies as well as others with colorful chord formations.

c. Tempo and volume. The Sunday anthems need a week-by-week contrast in tempo and volume, ranging from the sustained half notes of Palestrina's "We Adore Thee" to the syncopations of Martin Shaw's "With a Voice of Singing."

d. Range of difficulty. The average anthem should take about four rehearsals to prepare amply for performance. In addition to a good supply of anthems of this level of difficulty, the choir should have several others which are more easily attainable. These are especially useful for times when rehearsals are being largely devoted to a special musical program or a larger work. On the other hand, the choir will reach new musical heights if it is frequently challenged with more difficult works which may take several months to prepare.

e. Familiarity. No choral repertoire is complete without several well-known and well-liked numbers. These could be choral settings of familiar hymns, traditional anthems or gospel song arrangements.

3. *Explore the sources.* In conclusion, it will be helpful to establish ways in which a choral repertoire can be built. After the director has determined, through the preceding analysis, just what type of music is best suited for his choir, he must then seek out this music from the extensive materials available. Obviously, he could begin by visiting the local music store, where he would be permitted to peruse the many anthems that are in stock. However, the following suggestions may prove to be more helpful:

a. Attend church music conferences and workshops. By becoming a part of a reputable church music organization, such as the National Church Music Fellowship, the American Guild of Organists or the Choristers' Guild, he will be able to obtain several carefully selected lists of anthems. By attending local music workshops conducted by Christian colleges or publishers of sacred music, he will become acquainted with the latest publications, have opportunity to hear them and occasionally be able to obtain sample copies.

b. Write to several publishers. Upon request, most publishers of sacred music will provide the director with catalogs, lists and examination copies of music that is designed to meet his need. In writing for these, the particular level of difficulty and voice limitations should be indicated.

c. Learn to recognize reputable composers. When an anthem has proved successful in meeting his choir needs, the director should look for other music by the same composer. He should also examine the music of standard composers, such as those mentioned earlier in the chapter.

d. Consult other choir directors. In spite of the success of other methods of obtaining materials, the personal recommendation of another director is often the most dependable way.

Summary

As has been clearly established, the work of the adult church choir is an important one to the ministry of the church. Its effectiveness, however, is dependent on many factors. It must be staffed by dedicated laymen who see the work of the choir as a dynamic ministry. It must have good leadership, so that the program of progress will correspond with the desire for increased efficiency. It must have good materials to sing, in order that the message of the gospel will ring out clear and true. And finally it must be sanctioned and empowered by the Holy Spirit so that God can use its ministry to lead men and women into an experience of worship and draw unbelievers to a place of personal commitment to Christ.

RECOMMENDED READING

HALTER, C. *The Christian Choir Member*. St. Louis: Concordia Publishing House, 1959.

HEATON, C. H. *How to Build a Church Choir*. St. Louis: Bethany Press, 1958.

SATEREN, L. B. *The Good Choir*. Minneapolis: Augsburg Publishing House, 1963.

STEERE, D. *Music for the Protestant Church Choir*. Richmond: John Knox Press, 1955.

WILSON, H. R. and LYALL, J. L. *Building a Church Choir*. Minneapolis: Hall and McCreary, 1957.

Chapter 14

INSTRUMENTAL ENSEMBLES

Introduction

A survey of the average Sunday school and church membership will often disclose many present and former members of the local school band or orchestra. Despite this fact, churches have often neglected the area of instrumental ensembles in their music program. There are usually many reasons for this, several of which are discussed in this chapter. Yet the fact of the close relationship of the historical development of instruments to the historical background of worship, plus the fact that the church possesses musical talents that it is not utilizing in its program, makes this a vital subject for consideration.

Ever since the beginning of man's existence, he has attempted to make musical sounds. His first primitive attempts were those of beating on hollow logs, blowing over the open end of plant reeds and through animal horns. Later he discovered that other sounds could be obtained by stretching strands of animal hair across the end of a hollow log and causing them to vibrate by plucking or drawing a stick across them. As crude as they were, these discoveries brought about the birth of the three families of instruments used in symphony orchestras today: the percussions, winds and strings.

Instrumental Development in Bible Times

The Old Testament contains such detailed accounts of the development and use of musical instruments that the music historians Kurt Sachs and John Stainer have based much of their research on the Bible accounts. As far back as the time of Jubal, known as the "father of all such as handle the harp and organ" (Gen. 4:21), at least two families of instruments were having wide usage. These were the strings, known as the harp, and the wind instrument, called the organ.

One of the most important contributors to instrumental devel-

opment was the Psalmist David. In I Chronicles 23:5, he refers
to himself as a maker of instruments: "Four thousand praised
the Lord with the instruments which I made, said David, to praise
therewith." Other scriptures give more details as to the construction of some of these instruments and the many varieties found in
the three families of instrumentation. In view of the 'program of
instrumental music to be discussed, let us consider several of those
most frequently used.

1. *Strings.* Two great factors basic to present-day stringed instruments were discovered by David three thousand years ago.
He discovered that the type of string, plus the tension with which
it is attached, determines the pitch that will result. He also con-
cluded that the shape and size of the frame that holds the strings
determine the tone quality. Thus David laid the foundation for
a field of study considered to be a modern discovery—acoustics and
sound principles.

PSALTERY   KINNOR

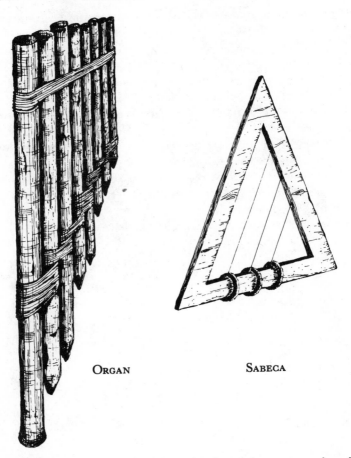

ORGAN   SABECA

There are three main varieties of stringed instruments found in the original Hebrew Bible:

a. The *kinnor* (Gen. 4:21), sometimes called the *gittith* (Ps. 8). It was a small instrument which was plucked by a plectrum or by the fingers, and was popular for accompanying the voice. It is described in Psalm 81:2 as a "pleasant" instrument. It denoted joy. In fact, it was this instrument that was placed among the willows when Israel was in captivity, indicating that joy had left the people (Ps. 137:2). Isaiah and Ezekiel both threatened to cease the sound of the *kinnor* when Israel sinned (Isa. 24:8; Ezek. 26:13).

b. The psaltery and the harp were practically synonymous and are referred to as the *nebhel*. This was more elaborate in size and more brilliant in tone than the *kinnor*. There were many different sizes and shapes, and there was no established number of strings that each instrument should have.

c. The *sabeca,* mentioned in Daniel 3:5-7, was a smaller instrument than the others and usually had three or four strings. This is the instrument often found pictured in ancient murals, usually held by women of ill repute.

2. *Wind instruments.* Wind instruments were originally made from hollow twigs, animal horns, or reeds from plants. The trumpet mentioned in Psalm 150 was an animal horn which produced tone when the player blew directly into it. The organ was a set of reeds which were blown across in the same manner in which the flute is played.

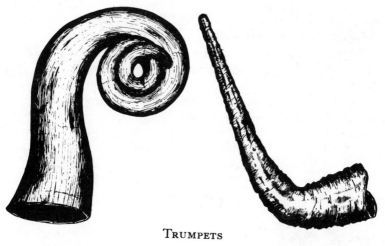

TRUMPETS

a. The trumpet family included the *keren,* the horn of an ox, ram or goat. It was played exclusively by priests for religious ceremonies, or by kings and military leaders to alert warriors or to announce a victory. In the German translation of the Bible, Luther used the German equivalent of the trombone when referring to ceremonial occasions, and the trumpet when speaking of military events. In Numbers 10:10, Moses ordered two silver trumpets (*keren*) to be used to call the assembly together, while the historian Josephus believed that there were as many as two hundred thousand used in temple worship during the time of David and Solomon. Other types of trumpets include the *shofar* (Lev. 25:9), probably the most brilliant, and the *yobel* (Exodus 19:13).

b. The organ, or pipe, was made from hollow twigs. Holes were bored into the sides to produce variances of pitch. These tonal

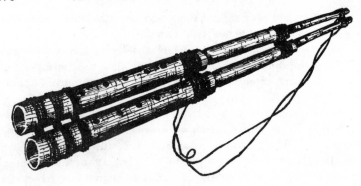

DOUBLE PIPE

effects were softer than those of the trumpet family, due to the way in which the instruments were blown.

c. The flute (*chalil*), found in Jeremiah 48:36, was used in mourning, or for soft accompaniment to the temple choirs (Ps. 87:7).

Another form of flute was called the *mashrokutha*, which was used for religious dances. This consisted of several pipes tied together.

FLUTE

3. *Percussions*. The Psalmist often referred to the timbrel and the dance concurrently.

a. The timbrel was a percussion instrument similar to a baby rattle. There were several varieties of these. They were encased or filled with stones to make a rattling sound. The timbrel family included the *toph,* called a *tabret* in Genesis 31:27. It was similar to a tambourine. Another type, the *menaanim,* looked and sounded like a castanet. The timbrel family did not establish a strong rhythm, but rather produced a clamorous noise.

b. The cymbal is also mentioned in Psalm 150. This was the loudest, most rhythmic type of percussion instrument used in David's day, and it was played by the music leaders to keep the choirs and other instruments together (I Chron. 15:19). It was usually a solid piece of metal, beaten upon with a hammer or the fist. Sometimes the cymbal consisted of an animal skin stretched across a hollow log or frame, much like our drums today. The cymbal family includes the *shalishim* found in I Samuel 18:6, and the *mesiltayim*, called *tseltslim* in II Samuel 6:5.

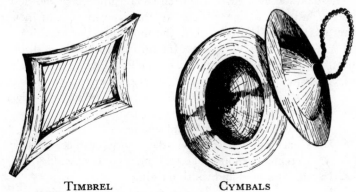

TIMBREL   CYMBALS

The Use of Instruments in Bible Times

Some of the numerous uses of musical instruments recorded in the Bible include:

1. In public ceremonies
    Joyous celebrations, tabret and harp (Gen. 31:27).
    Anointing of kings, trumpets and pipes (I Kings 1:39; II Chron. 23:13).
2. In relation to battles
    Gideon's army, trumpets (Judges 7:16-23).
    Miriam's song of victory, timbrels (Exod. 15:20).
    The song of David's victory, tabrets and others (I Sam. 18:6).
3. In religious festivities
    Removal of the ark from Gibeah, all instruments (II Sam. 6:5).
    The ark to Jerusalem, all instruments (I Chron. 15:28; 16:5).
    Dedication of the temple, all instruments (II Chron. 5:12, 13).
    Foundation of second temple laid, trumpets and cymbals (Ezra 3:10).
    Dedication of the wall of Jerusalem, cymbals, psalteries and harps (Neh. 12:27).

4. Instrumental instructors
    Jubal, harp and organ (Gen. 4:21).
    Heman, Asaph and Ethan, cymbals, psalteries, harps
        and trumpets (I Chron. 15); also Jeduthun (16:42).

Values of an Instrumental Program Today

The question as to why a church should undertake the development of instrumental groups can be answered in light of their two ministries: to the church and to the individual participating.

1. Ministry to the church. Instrumental groups add interest and freshness to the music program of the church. There are many different ways in which they can be used to enrich the services.

a. In preludes, offertories and postludes, taking the place of the organ, or accompanying or assisting the organ.

b. To accompany congregational singing.

c. For special music selections in the services or in concerts.

d. To accompany choirs, solos and other vocal ensembles.

e. In Sunday school and youth meetings.

f. In street meetings, outdoor services and rescue missions.

g. For social and recreational events.

2. Ministry to the participant. As is the case with all the other musical organizations, the instrumental groups minister to the participants just as much as they do to the services of the church. Instrumental groups offer opportunities for wholesome activity, Christian fellowship, and nurturing and developing talents that doubtless would not be utilized through the choir programs. In many instances they are welcome opportunities for men and women to use the instruments they purchased for use in the school orchestra or band many years before. This aspect of participation makes these groups evangelistic efforts as well, since they often attract those who have not made a personal commitment of their lives to Christ. The nature of the activity is different enough from the leadership ministry of the adult choir so that it is possible to use the instrumental groups as means of attracting the unchurched, thus establishing a contact with the church which may lead to an acceptance of Christ as personal Saviour. Another ministry is the nurture and development of the Christian who participates in the effort of winning these people for Christ.

Membership in Instrumental Groups

The requirements for membership in all instrumental groups should be similar to those of the choirs, but there are a few necessary differences.

1. Age requirements. The age span can be more inclusive, since physical maturity does not affect instrumental proficiency as much as it does the vocal. Since there will no doubt be a large variety of instruments available, a wider age span may be necessary to maintain a balance of instrumentation in the groups.

2. Musical qualifications. The performance ability of an instrumentalist must be high. While choir members become integral parts of a group who are singing only a few parts, most instrumentalists have independent parts to play; thus poor ability becomes more apparent. Consequently, one of the following programs should be considered:

a. Organize two groups, one for training and the other for performance, with provisions for advancement when qualifications can be met.

b. Establish a probationary membership, permitting the less advanced to rehearse regularly with the group, but not to perform until probationary restrictions are lifted by the director.

3. Moral and spiritual life. As has already been mentioned, this type of ministry seems to lend itself to an inner evangelistic program. Therefore nonbelievers can be encouraged to take part. This is not the case in the adult choir where certain precautions must be exercised to prevent jeopardizing its ministry of leadership. On the other hand, there should be no lowering of standards of moral conduct within these groups.

Organizational Structure

An instrumental program is a difficult one to structure. The number of groups and kinds of combinations must depend entirely upon the instruments available. The accompanying table suggests several types of ensembles, both large and small, which can be used in a church instrumental program. Based on these combinations, there are four plans which may be followed in setting up the organizational structure.

First plan, involving a well-balanced complement of strings and other orchestral instruments:

Full orchestra, as indicated on the table. It is desirable to maintain as good a balance of instruments as possible, determining the balance largely by the string section. For example, if there is only a minimum number of strings, all other sections should be restricted to the designated minimum.

Brass choir, reed ensemble and other necessary combinations to accommodate the other instruments.

TABLE OF INSTRUMENTAL COMBINATIONS

Orchestra		*Concert Band*	
Strings:	4 to 12 violins (I and II) 1 to 4 violas 1 to 4 cellos 1 to 3 string basses	Reeds:	2 to 4 flutes 1 or 2 oboes 2 to 4 clarinets 1 or 2 bassoons 0 or 1 bass clarinet
Reeds:	1 or 2 flutes 0 or 1 oboe 2 clarinets 0 or 1 bassoon	Brass:	2 to 4 French horns 2 or 3 trumpets 3 or 4 trombones 1 or 2 baritones 0 or 1 tuba
Brass:	1 or 2 French horns 2 trumpets 1 or 3 trombones		
Piano and harp: optional			

Brass Choir	*Reed Quintet*
2 to 6 trumpets or cornets 1 to 3 French horns 1 to 3 trombones 1 or 2 baritones (or trombones) 0 or 1 tuba	flute, oboe, clarinet, French horn, bassoon *Larger Reed Ensemble* Equal number of each of the above, plus piccolo, English horn and bass clarinet

String Ensembles	*Brass Quartets*
Choir: approximate balance as in orchestra Quartet: 2 violins, viola, cello	2 trumpets, 2 trombones trumpet, alto, trombone, baritone

Small combinations: trumpet trio, French horn quartet, flute trio, trombone trio, string ensemble with reed solo, reed ensemble with brass solo

Second plan, involving a good balance of reeds and brass, but not enough strings:

Concert band as indicated, seeking to balance parts according to the number of reeds available.

Brass choir, string ensemble and other groups as necessary.

Third plan, involving many instruments, but not well balanced:

Brass choir or ensemble, reed quintet or ensemble and other groups as necessary.

Fourth plan, involving only a few miscellaneous instruments:

Organize any small groups possible, utilizing other instruments in solos, obbligato parts, duets and in other ways.

Possible Substitutions

It is possible to substitute certain instruments for others, sometimes even from different families, as long as there is no appreciable change in quality or balance. Some common substitutions are:

Piccolo for flute

English horn for oboe or clarinet

Saxophone for clarinet, bassoon or trombone

Bass clarinet for bassoon or tuba

Alto horn for French horn or trombone

Baritone horn or euphonium for trombone or tuba

In many of the above substitutions, parts will need to be transposed. In others, the suggestions depend upon the range of the music involved.

Rehearsals

All instrumental ensembles should have specific times for rehearsal each week, or no less frequently than every two weeks. The rehearsals should follow the general pattern previously set for choral groups.

Repertoire

Although there is an increasing number of sacred works being published for instruments, it is still rather difficult to find music to suit every combination. The following sources are suggested:

1. Published instrumental settings.

a. Standard works by composers such as Purcell, Bach and others, originally written for or adapted to instrumental groups.

b. Instrumental parts accompanying standard hymnals. These are provided by several publishers of hymnals.

c. Arrangements of sacred works. Many of these are arranged

in four, five or six parts which can be adapted to almost any instrumental combinations.

d. Accompaniments for anthems, cantatas and oratorios. Those available, either by rental or purchase, will be indicated on the choral scores.

2. *Other music which can be adapted.*

a. Anthems, either the vocal parts, the accompaniments, or both.

b. Piano and organ solos. The difficulty in arranging these would be the possible inconsistency in voicing.

c. Vocal duets, trios and quartets, for smaller ensembles.

The greatest problems in adapting vocal or keyboard music are those of transposing for the various instruments and selecting music which is appropriately pitched for the instruments.

Handbell Choirs

A rather recent development in American churches, which has come from long traditions in Europe, is the use of handbells. This is an excellent means of teaching rhythm and coordination to both adults and children. Although the cost of a good set of handbells is high, it should be a worthwhile investment for the church to make. It will also contribute refreshing variety to the musical program of the church.

Handbell sets usually consist of twenty-five, thirty-two or thirty-seven bells, spanning from two to three octaves chromatically. The choir personnel may consist of as few as ten members. Each player is usually assigned two bells, with three or four assigned to the players of the extreme high and low notes. The church which has purchased a set would be wise to organize several choirs, perhaps on a graded plan, consisting of members of regular vocal groups or serving as a training group for future choir members.

1. Usage. For preludes, offertories, postludes and special selections; for accompanying children's and women's voices.

2. Repertoire. Music is provided for handbells through most publishers of sacred music. However, many hymn tunes can be used as written or with occasional addition of chords. Information concerning methods, materials and ways of forming such groups may be obtained through the American Guild of English Handbell Ringers or the Choristers' Guild.

Using Other Instruments

It is not easy to devise ways of using all instruments in the church. Nonorchestral instruments, such as accordions and guitars, or those which do not lend themselves to solos or church music, such as drums, piccolos and tubas, are often neglected because of their limitations. To encourage active use of these instruments, the following suggestions should be considered:

1. Conduct an occasional "talent night" program on a week-night, in which young and old are encouraged to participate, using both standard secular works and sacred songs.

2. Have an occasional youth participation night on a Sunday, emphasizing the fact that it is designed to use all youth who can sing or play. The program may be planned so that it concludes with several selections of musical quality and spiritual depth.

3. Use talent in conjunction with youth fellowships or socials. Instruments such as the accordion or guitar may even be used to accompany the informal singing of folk songs at such functions.

Conclusion

Although this may be the most flexible or perhaps even the most unpredictable area in the church music program, it is essential that all who play instruments should be given opportunities to use their talents for the Lord. Realizing that this is often the most difficult department to administer and for which to provide materials, it is hoped that the suggestions in this chapter will be practical and helpful in attempting to fulfill this need.

SUGGESTED READING

McCOMMON, P. *Music in the Bible*. Nashville: Convention Press, 1956.

SACHS, KURT. *The History of Musical Instruments*. New York: Norton and Company, 1940.

STAINER, JOHN. *The Music of the Bible*. London: Novello and Company, 1914.

SYDNOR, J. R. *Planning for Church Music*. Nashville: Abingdon Press, 1961.

TROBIAN, H. R. *The Instrumental Ensemble in the Church*. Nashville: Abingdon Press, 1963.

TUFTS, N. P. *The Art of Handbell Ringing*. Nashville: Abingdon Press, 1961.

WATSON, DORIS. *The Handbell Choir*. New York: H. W. Gray Company, 1959.

Chapter 15

PHYSICAL EQUIPMENT

Introduction

It is a fact that many churches conduct commendable programs of choirs, congregational singing and instrumental ensembles with little more than a piano, a few chairs and some hymnals in the sanctuary. The inability to procure equipment does not prohibit a church from maintaining such a program. However, it is obvious that there will always be limitations to its development under such circumstances. A music ministry will never reach its highest potential unless certain basic rehearsal equipment is available and acoustics are conducive to performance. A financial investment in the improvement and expansion of facilities will invariably pay for itself in an improved and expanded ministry. The better the equipment, the greater the potential.

The following outline indicates the facilities which are necessary for a complete graded choir and instrumental program. In studying the list, three things should be observed:

1. The suggested equipment has been chosen conservatively to stay within the budget of a medium-sized church, therefore should be considered as minimal requirements.

2. To keep within the budget, it is often necessary to begin by obtaining the most needed equipment. A long-range plan should then be developed which would provide for additional purchases and improvements each year for a number of years.

3. A smaller program will not demand all the equipment indicated.

FACILITIES NEEDED FOR AN AVERAGE CHURCH MUSIC PROGRAM

In the Sanctuary

Choir loft, plus other platform space suitable for choirs and instrumental ensembles; organ and/or piano; conductor's stand and podium; hymnals.

In the Rehearsal Rooms*

Piano; straight-backed, movable chairs; music stands; blackboard and bulletin board; coat and hat racks (or accessibility to same); storage space for instruments, music stands and rehearsal equipment; table or racks for placing music to be used; periodical stand and/or bookshelf for reading material.

Robe Facilities*

Closets for storing robes; mirrors; coat and hat racks (or accessibility to same); accessibility to space for changing into robes and rest room facilities.

Library Equipment*

Legal-sized files for organ, piano and orchestral scores; files or shelves for choral and solo music; shelves or closet space for large collections of music, hymnals, oratorios and cantatas; card file for reference to music on file; sorting table or racks.

Office Facilities*

Desk, chairs, files and bookshelves for minister of music; typewriter; accessibility to duplicating or mimeographing equipment.

The Choir Loft

There are three paramount factors which must be considered in building an ideal choir loft:

(1) It should be in a position where it can project the sound equally to all parts of the congregation. (2) It should provide maximum satisfaction to the choir when singing. (3) It should be situated in such a way that it does not detract from worship.

These factors are largely determined by the location, seating arrangement and acoustical surroundings.

1. Location. According to traditional practices, the theological position of a church and its concept of worship are important factors in determining the location of its choir loft. In all instances, the choir is supposed to be facing the "central part of worship," which is either the altar or the pulpit, depending upon the church's theological emphasis. If the function of the choir in the worship service is primarily to minister *to* the congregation, as is true in many nonliturgical churches, the choir loft is usually situated in the front of the sanctuary, in the chancel, facing the congregation.

---

* The above facilities may all be located in one room if desired, but should be separated from the sanctuary.

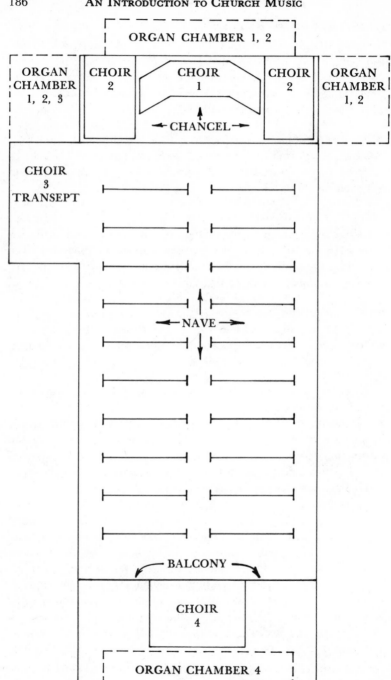

If, however, the choir's task is basically that of leading and representing the people, it is sometimes located in the balcony or in a transept, and is facing the minister. A present-day trend in many churches is for the choir to function almost equally in both capacities. As a result, there has also been an increased trend toward the use of the transept for a choir loft, since it is in close proximity to the chancel, yet is still identifiable with the congregation.

As indicated in the diagram, there are four generally accepted locations for the church choir loft. From the standpoint of musical and functional effectiveness, each has its advantages and disadvantages. These may be summarized as follows:

a. Front of sanctuary, center of chancel. This is one of the best positions for sound projection, but it can be distracting to worship if it is not at the proper elevation. If it is above the height of the pulpit, nearly every motion of the choir members will be seen. The ideal level is slightly below or even with the pulpit, strategically arranged so that the choir is not in plain view when seated, yet can be seen and heard when standing.

b. Front of sanctuary, side of chancel. There are two types of side locations.

(1) The divided choir loft, with half the choir on either side of the chancel, facing toward the center. The tone of the two sections mixes in the middle of the chancel, somewhat on the principle of stereophonic sound resulting from two equalized speakers located on two sides of a room. The results can be very effective when each side is balanced within itself. The disadvantages are: the lack of direct contact with the congregation when singing, resulting in an appreciable loss of diction and expression, and the problems of precision and blend between the two sides, especially with amateur singers who tend to depend upon one another.

(2) The choir loft on one side only. This arrangement is more practical for amateur choir members, in that it gives them a greater sense of unity as well as making it easier for them to hear their own blend. There are three ways in which the seats may be arranged:

(a) Facing the center of the chancel, sidewise to the congregation. Again, this will result in a lack of communication with the congregation, but will also suffer from the lack of circulation of tone.

(b) Facing the congregation, directly forward. This will improve the communication and will be most effective in a long sanctuary, but it may result in poor contact with one side of the congregation if the sanctuary is especially wide.

(c) Facing the center of the sanctuary. Although it may be difficult to arrange in certain architectural situations, this position provides the best congregational contact of any of the three.

c. Side of sanctuary, transept. This type of choir loft is usually located in a small section, called a transept, near the front of the sanctuary, though not a part of the sanctuary proper. This arrangement will minimize the amount of attention drawn to the choir and yet provide good congregational contact. The seating arrangement must be centralized so that the voices will project to the entire congregation.

d. Balcony. If a congregation has been accustomed to being able to see all those taking part in music, there may be objections to a balcony location. However, this situation has many advantages. Well centralized, it will provide an excellent projection of tone, blend, diction and expression, with little or no distraction to worship. Choir directors frequently prefer it because they are not such public spectacles when conducting. The only problem of reception will occur when part of the congregation is seated underneath the balcony.

2. *The seating.* Seats in the choir loft should be straight-backed and unpadded, unless plastic or other nonabsorbent material is used. If the rows are long, they should be curved at each end, as indicated in location number *1* on the diagram. For an average capacity of thirty to forty singers, three or four rows are preferred. Each row should be elevated four to eight inches above the row in front of it. Racks should be located in front of each seat for choir music and hymnals. Lighting and ventilation should be good.

3. *The acoustics.* The balance and blend of good choral tone are dependent largely upon the start they get. To provide the best start possible, the choir loft should be of a shell-type design, with hard-surfaced walls—preferably hardwood paneling or plaster—on either side, and a rather low ceiling. Both ceiling and walls should expand out into the sanctuary proper.

Acoustical count should be about 2.6 seconds vibration. To obtain this, the choir loft should be kept relatively free from absorbent materials found in drapes, seat padding and carpeting. If, however, an unpleasant echo occurs (judgment must be based on a full or nearly full congregation), some may be added. Drapery should seldom be placed near the front of the choir loft, and carpeting should never be underneath the choir when singing, but rather in the aisles.

The Organ

There are many sides to the frequently discussed question as to whether the church should purchase a pipe organ or an electronic instrument. The decision should be based on an equal consideration of the following factors.

1. Cost. A pipe organ is more expensive not only to purchase but also to maintain, since it is advisable to tune and service it at least three times a year. Churches which cannot spend eight thousand dollars or more for a new instrument would do well to consider an electronic organ.

2. Space. In purchasing a small-sized (six- to eight-rank) pipe organ, the church must be able to provide space for about 450 to 500 pipes, to be placed in a chamber or expression box with a tone opening of about nine feet in width and seven feet in height. Some of the ranks may be mounted in front of the chamber, which would result in greater strength and presence of tone, but might impose slight limitations on the expressiveness of the instrument. Space must also be provided for blowers inside the chamber and a motor in another part of the church building, with conduits running from the motor room to the chamber, and from the chamber to the console.

Electronic speakers do not demand as much space, but will produce a more satisfactory tone if they can also be encased in chambers, provided the tone opening is comparable to the above specifications. Conduits must again be provided from the chamber to the console.

The console will require from four to six square feet of floor space, depending on the size of the instrument.

3. Location. Speakers or pipes should be installed so that the tone will provide good support to the choir and also project into the entire sanctuary with the least possible obstruction. The diagram shows how they should relate to the choir loft. (The numbers correspond with the numbers of the various loft positions.) The installation should be quite high and, according to the National Council of Churches' pamphlet *The Church Organ*, the tone should be able to travel unhindered in three directions.

The console should be in proximity to the front of the choir, especially if it is played by a combined organist-director. It should also be situated so that the organist can see the pulpit and the rear of the nave, either directly or by mirror.

4. Acoustics and size of sanctuary. Normally a church with a seating capacity of more than two hundred fifty will require a

larger organ than the one suggested above. However, it is to be remembered that organs are constructed of brick and mortar as well as pipes or speakers. The amount of sound-absorbing factors, such as high ceilings, porous cement blocks, acoustical tile, excess pillars, unusual architectural designs, as well as the previously mentioned absorbent materials in drapes and carpeting, determine how the organ will sound. The ideal reverberation time for an auditorium in which both speaking and music are of equal importance is about two seconds or less when the auditorium is comfortably filled. If the auditorium is unusually dead, it is advisable to purchase a pipe organ rather an electronic one, as the pipe organ can be voiced to compensate for the lack of sound reflection, whereas the direct, penetrating sound which results from an electronic speaker will only be magnified by the poor acoustics.

5. Musical needs. A church must invest in the finest organ within its means, if it desires to have a fully developed music program of all styles of choral and organ repertoire, oratorio and cantata performances, sacred artist recitals and good congregational singing. The extent of the musical program should be an even greater factor than the size of the church, when determining the size instrument that should be purchased.

The Piano

1. Size and make. The sanctuary piano should be a grand, ranging from five feet eight inches to seven feet in length. It is possible for a church seating less than two hundred to use a smaller size grand. If, however, the seating capacity is over eight hundred, or the auditorium is excessively large or acoustically poor, the nine-foot concert model should be considered. It is neither wise nor practical to invest in an unknown make unless it is highly recommended by someone who understands piano construction. Often a good rebuilt piano will be both more serviceable and less expensive than a new instrument.

2. Location. The keyboard should be located to the left of the congregation so that the tone will project into the sanctuary. If it is used for accompanying the choir, it should also be close to the choir loft.

3. Service. All church pianos should be tuned and inspected every six months, or even more frequently if they are subjected to constant changes in room temperatures.

The Rehearsal Rooms

1. The choir room. This room should be large enough to accommodate twice the number of persons normally using it. It must be well ventilated, and should have individual controls for adjusting the heat. Lighting should be adequate for close reading. The acoustics in the singing area of the room should be very reflective, while the conductor's half should be considerably less.

Facilities for coats, rehearsal supplies and rhythm instruments should be within the room or in an adjoining room or closet. The music library, robing room and rest rooms should be nearby, and the sanctuary should be accessible, yet far enough away, or the walls sufficiently soundproof, to permit preservice rehearsals.

The seats should be movable, so as to implement various changes in the rehearsal arrangements as well as to adapt to various size groups. If the room is used by children's choirs, small-sized chairs should be available. All seats should be equipped with music holders.

The piano should either be a small grand or a forty-five-inch studio upright.

2. Instrumental rehearsal room. When rehearsing groups which include wind instruments, a large room is necessary, with acoustics which approximate those of the sanctuary. If a large enough room cannot be provided, it is best to practice in the sanctuary. Sometimes it is possible to use the choir room, but only if the instrumental group is quite small, or if the room is larger than previously specified.

The most vital needs are storage closets for instruments and music stands, and accessibility to the music library or a special file for the instrumental music in the rehearsal room.

Handbell choirs and string ensembles will rehearse best in the room prepared for vocal groups, but will need additional storage space for music stands, bells and larger stringed instruments.

Choir Robes and Robe Closets

Most cap and gown companies provide robes in nearly every price range, but the lowest priced fabrics are not always too durable. The most practical type of material is a wrinkle-resistant, lightweight cloth of conservative color which will not fade.

Dust-free robe closets should be built into the walls of the rehearsal room, or an adjoining robing room should be available, with space provided for changing into the robes, several large wall mirrors, facilities for coats and hats, lockers for purses and other valuables, and nearby rest room facilities. All robes should be numbered and possibly have names attached. The number should correspond to the position in the closet. A list including names and robe numbers should be posted on the bulletin board for easy reference. If several sets of robes are stored in the same room, it is advisable to identify each with a letter representing the choir, similar to the library filing system to be discussed next. The bulletin board would then read:

ADULT CHOIR	WOMEN'S ENSEMBLE
Jones, Mary E26	Smith, Catherine C15

Most good choir robes will not need to be cleaned more than once a year, unless the color is exceptionally light. Stoles, surplices and collars should be cleaned or washed more frequently.

The Music Library

1. Filing of music. All music should be marked and filed according to voice or instrument classification, using a letter code as follows:

A=Children's choirs (s. [soprano] and s.a. [soprano, alto])

B=Youth choirs (s.a.b. [soprano, alto, baritone])

C=Women's voices (s.s.a. [two sopranos, one alto] and s.s.a.a. [two sopranos, two altos])

D=Men's voices (t.t.b.b. [two tenors, two basses])

E=Mixed choirs (s.a.t.b. and divided)

F=Multiple choirs (all combinations)

G=Orchestra, band, instrumental groups

H=Handbell choir

Suggested steps for processing new music would be:

a. Stamp the code and anthem number on every copy.

b. File in a 9x15 manila folder bearing the same letter and number and place in a legal-sized file drawer. Since it is usually difficult to file music alphabetically without having to make frequent revisions of the drawer contents, a suggested procedure is to number the music in sequence of purchase, and file it accordingly.

c. Prepare two 4x6 file cards, to be filed according to composer and name of anthem. These cards should include the file code and number, the voicing, number of copies purchased and particular usage (Advent, Christmas, general, etc.).

Sample of composer card   Sample of title card

Bach, J. S. E 215	"All Ye Good People" A 45
"Now Let Every Tongue Adore Thee"	Kountz
SATB G. Schirmer	SA Galaxy
35 copies Advent,	40 copies Christmas
General	

When the director or librarian wants an anthem, he may look in the file under the composer or title. The accompanying file code will identify its place in the files. If desired, the dates on which each anthem is used may be recorded on the back of the cards.

2. *Storing of cantatas, oratorios and large collections.* Larger items may be filed similarly to the other music, or can be stored on regular library shelves with labels placed underneath the books for identification.

The Hymnal

One of the most essential parts of the church music equipment is the hymnal, the most frequently used book in public worship. Choosing a hymnal is no easy task. It involves a large investment, usually costing several hundred dollars just to supply the average sanctuary.

1. *Hymnal contents.* It is important to assess the contents which will be needed to maintain the type of music program the church desires. The following four factors must be considered:

a. Hymnody. A good all-purpose hymnal should contain at least five hundred well-selected hymns for congregational singing. These should include:

(1) An abundant supply of worship hymns.

(2) Songs of personal testimony and experience.

(3) A wide assortment of hymns on subjects such as commitment, holiness of life, invitation, judgment, justification, missions, prayer, security and the second coming of Christ.

(4) Seasonal hymns for Advent, Christmas, New Year, Passion Week, Easter, Pentecost, Thanksgiving; hymns for special occasions, such as funerals, memorials, dedications and weddings.

(5) Hymns and choruses directed to youth and children, with texts capable of ministering on their levels of understanding as well as elevating their minds and thoughts. This need may best be met by the use of a youth hymnal in the Sunday school and in other youth activities.

(6) Many tried and proved hymns which have enhanced the church's worship in the past, including those which are considered favorites.

(7) Several new or less familiar hymns, to provide for fresh worship experiences in the future.

It is important that these hymns be carefully examined to be sure that they are doctrinally sound and in accord with the denominational practices and beliefs of the local church.

b. Service music. In addition to the congregational music, the hymnal should contain at least a dozen responses (opening, prayer, offertory and benedictory) to be sung by the choir or congregation. These should include the Doxology and the Gloria Patri. The hymnal should also contain several easy selections for the choir, plus many hymns that can be adapted for choir use, with optional descants.

c. Other service material. There should be at least seventy-five to one hundred responsive reading selections based on varied subjects for general use and special seasons and occasions. It is also desirable to have several "calls to worship" to be used by the minister, as well as other scriptural helps and references for other uses.

d. Indexing. Some well-qualified hymns are rendered ineffective because of poor indexing. For easy access to hymns, the following indexes are necessary:

(1) A table of contents in the front of the hymnal, giving general classifications and divisions.

(2) An alphabetical index at the back, giving both titles and first lines of first stanzas.

(3) A topical index with all hymns classified under subject headings, such as adoration, consecration, faith. In order to be completely effective, the index should include at least three hundred different topics, with each hymn appearing in two or more topical classifications.

(4) Indexes of tunes and meters, designed to assist in finding alternate tunes to use with other texts.

(5) An index of authors, composers and sources, with respective dates and periods.

(6) An index of responsive readings and other scriptural helps contained in the hymnal, classified topically, alphabetically and by their biblical source references.

2. *Other factors to consider.* Careful thought should be given to the construction and durability of the hymnal, since it will be

used for many years, perhaps with rather rough handling at times. These factors should be considered:

a. Print. It is advisable to compare the print and engraving of several hymnals. One will immediately notice the difference in clarity of notes and letters, in the evenness of ink distribution and in the alignment of margins.

b. Paper. The quality of paper may be the most difficult for the layman to determine, since the only true test of quality is time. Heavy paper is not always the best grade of paper. The best test is whether or not the ink shows through on the other side. It is also important that the grain of the paper run vertically on the page. Horizontal grain will cause the pages to stand straight up when the book is open. If the grain runs in the right direction, the pages will fan easily. A smooth-grain paper will resist fingerprints and will not tend to turn yellow after years of usage. Perhaps a visit to a church which has been using the hymnal will be the best way to determine its quality and endurance.

c. Cover. Most cloth, except linen, will give good service. The best service, however, will be gotten from a fabrikoid cover.

d. Binding. A loose binding is preferred, as there is less possibility of the spine of the book breaking. The regular thread-sewn binding is not sufficient to withstand the abuse an average hymnal receives. Therefore it is advisable to see that the first and last sections are reinforced with a cambric strip. The top and bottom should also be headbanded for maximum protection. The added expense for these precautions is only slight, and will assure a longer life for the hymnals.

3. *Extra features.* It is good to have the name of the church engraved on the hymnals. This should be done in an untarnishable gold finish.

If possible, spiral or loose-leaf editions should be obtained for the piano and organ. Orchestrations should also be purchased if orchestral instruments are used in the church services.

4. *Youth hymnals.* Normally, the church hymnal is used for all services. However, it is often advisable to purchase hymnals prepared especially for the youth, to be used in Sunday school and other Christian education work. These hymnals should be carefully chosen to meet the needs of the departments in which they will be used. They should include many of the standard hymns of the church, but should also contain hymns and choruses designed for particular ages. The most important feature of these hymnals

is the indexing of all hymns according to age groupings, making it easy to select music for each department.

5. *Hymnals for the home.* When hymnals are purchased for the church or Christian education department, members of the church should be encouraged to obtain copies for home use. These could be ordered along with the church hymnals at a considerable saving. However, in order to avoid confusion, it is advisable to order family copies in a color different from those used in the church.

General Suggestions Concerning Physical Equipment

1. When purchasing new equipment. Seek the counsel of several people who understand the instrument or product. Buy with expansion in view. Purchase the most durable materials possible.

2. When building or remodeling the church. Ask the architect to consult an organ builder for exact specifications for organ chamber space, motor room, conduits and tone opening. Consult a lighting engineer for advice on illumination needed for practice rooms and sanctuary. Consult an acoustical technician for advice on materials to use for wall construction, paneling, carpeting and other accessories, showing him the architect's proposals to get his reaction to the plans of the sanctuary and rehearsal rooms. Be sure that adequate library, closet and rehearsal space is provided for an expanding music program. Visit and observe the facilities of other churches which have a larger program in music.

SUGGESTED READING

Blanton, J. *The Organ in Church Design.* Albany, Tex.: Venture Press, 1957.

Lovelace, A. C. and Rice, W. C. *Music and Worship in the Church.* Nashville: Abingdon Press, 1960.

Sydnor, J. R. *Planning for Church Music.* Nashville: Abingdon Press, 1961.

APPENDIX

Unison Anthems Suitable for Children's Choirs

Title	Composer	Publisher
A Song of Praise	Thiman	Banks and Son
A Thanksgiving Hymn	Thiman	Mills
Blessed Man Whom God Doth Aid	Lovelace	J. Fischer
Brother James's Air	arr. Jacob	Oxford
Christmas Song	Holst	G. Schirmer
Gesu Bambino	Yon	J. Fischer
Hosanna, Lord	Clokey	Flammer
Jesus Was Born in Bethlehem	Marshall	C. Fischer
Kindly Spring Again Is Here	Lovelace	J. Fischer
My Heart Ever Faithful	Bach	E. C. Schirmer
O Saviour Sweet	Bach	Gray
Sabbath Bells	Stainer	Flammer
Sing Praises to God	Williams	Flammer
The Lamb	Smart	Hope
The Lord My Pasture Shall Prepare	Shaw	Novello
The Saints of God	Reed	C. Fischer
This Is Easter Day	Marryott	Ditson
We Praise Thee, O God	Willan	Concordia

Two-Part Anthems Suitable for Children's Choirs

Come, Together Let Us Sing	Bach	E. C. Schirmer
Easter Bell Carol	Davies	Flammer
Father, at Thy Throne We Bow	Rains	Hope
For the Blessings of Our Days	Krones	Kjos
God, Make My Life a Shining Light	Lovelace	Flammer
Good Shepherd of the Children	Hokanson	Kjos
I Will Sing New Songs	Dvorak	G. Schirmer
In the Bleak Mid Winter	Smart	Hope
Let All Things Now Living	Davis	E. C. Schirmer
Lord of All, to Thee We Pray	Grieg-Hirt	Witmark

197

My Shepherd	Bach-Hirt	Witmark
Nowell, Sing We Clear	Smart	Hope
O Saviour, Hear Me	Gluck-Ehret	Boosey & Hawkes
Prayer of the Norwegian Child	Kountz	G. Schirmer
The Flute Carol	Couper	J. Fischer
The Song of Praise	Brahms	Novello
The Wise May Bring Their Learning	Mueller	C. Fischer
Three Seasonal Anthems	Smart	Hope
Wondrous Love	Groom	Hope

Collections Suitable for Children's Choirs

Anthems for Junior Choristers	A. C. Lovelace	Summy-Birchard
Belfry Book	K. K. Davis	Remick
Descants for Christmas	B. & M. Krones	Kjos
Green Hill Anthem Book		E. C. Schirmer
Hymn Arrangements #5	Don Hustad	Hope
Junior Choir Praise	J. F. Wilson	Hope
Junior Chorus Choir	R. Prillwitz	Moody
Let Children Sing	M. Licht	Flammer
Unison Hymns with Descants	M. Pooler	Augsburg

Anthems in Three Parts (soprano, alto, baritone)

Christ the Lord Is Risen Today	Coggin	Hope
Crown Him with Many Crowns	Cain	Flammer
Fairest Lord Jesus	Hustad	Hope
God Is My Strong Salvation	Powell	Augsburg
Holy Is the Lord Our God	Vogler-Nevin	J. Fischer
Let All the Seas and Earth Around	Pitcher	Summy-Birchard
Lift Up Your Heads	Krapf	Augsburg
Now Let Every Tongue Adore Thee	Bach-Cain	Kjos
O Saving Victim	Pasquet	Augsburg
Our God Is a Rock	Davis	Summy-Birchard
Praise to God, Immortal Praise	Hoppin	Summy-Birchard
Praise Ye the Lord, the Almighty	Gesangbuch	Hall & McCreary
Shepherd of Tender Youth	Darst	Summy-Birchard
Stand Up, and Bless the Lord	Coggin	Hope
Throned Upon the Awful Tree	Running	Augsburg
To Thee We Sing	Tkach	Kjos
We Thank Thee, Lord	Tkach	Kjos

Anthems for Combined Choirs
(unison and SATB, unless otherwise indicated)

All Things Bright and Beautiful	Vleugel	Choral Services
Alleluia	Palestrina-Wright	Flammer
Be Thou My Vision	Pooler	Augsburg
Blessed Jesus	Christiansen	Augsburg
Carol of the Questioning Child	Kountz	G. Schirmer
Gift of Love	Posegate	Shawnee
Gloria in Excelsis	Jolley	Shawnee
Hosanna	arr. Bitgood	Gray
Joy Dawned Again on Easter Day	Bitgood	Gray
Let Hearts Awake and Sing (Adult, youth and children's choirs)	arr. Young	Kjos
O Bless Our God, Ye People	arr. Schroth	Kjos
O Tell Me, Children Dear	arr. Clokey	Birchard
Sing Gloria (SATB and SA)	Davis	Remick
Still, Still, Still (Unison, treble and mixed choirs)	arr. Young	Kjos

Practical Anthems for the Adult Choir for Each Sunday of the Church Year

Selections are coded as follows: E, easy; M, moderately difficult; D, difficult.

Communion Sunday

Jesu, Word of God Incarnate	Mozart	Gray	M
O Lamb of God (Agnus Dei)	Kalinnikof	Boston	M

Reformation

A Mighty Fortress	I uther-Cain	Schmitt, Hall, McCreary	M

Memorial Service and All Saints Day

For All the Saints	Vaughan Williams	C. Fischer	E
Behold the Host	Grieg	G. Schirmer	M

Thanksgiving or General

Praise, My Soul, the King of Heaven	Clokey	Flammer	E
For the Beauty of the Earth	arr. Hustad	Hope	M
For the Blessings of Our Days	arr. Krones	Kjos	E

Advent (Sundays Preceding Christmas)

Cherubim Song (No. 7)	Bortnyansky	C. Schirmer	E
Lo, How a Rose E'er Blooming	Praetorious	Gray	E
O Come, O Come, Emmanuel	Candlyn	Gray	M

Christmas

Break Forth, O Beauteous, Heavenly Light	Bach	E. C. Schirmer	M
Shepherds Loud Their Praises Singing	Rowley	Oxford	M

New Year's and Sundays Following

Rejoice, the Lord Is King	Darwell-Pfohl	Flammer	M
Now Let Every Tongue Adore Thee	Bach	E. C. Schirmer	E
Now Let Us All Praise God and Sing	Young	Galaxy	E

Universal Week of Prayer and Epiphany

Lead Me, Lord	Wesley	Wood	E
Open Now Thy Gates of Beauty	Wilson	Hoffman	M
Send Out Thy Spirit	Schuetky	Gray	
Bless the Lord, O My Soul	Ippolitoff-Ivanoff	G. Schirmer	E

Lenten Season

Jesu, Friend of Sinners	Grieg	Gray	M
O Sacred Head	Bach-Christiansen	Augsburg	M
Sweet the Moments, Rich in Blessing	arr. Ehret	Schmitt, Hall, McCreary	M
Go to Dark Gethsemane	Noble	Gray	D

Palm Sunday

All Glory, Laud and Honor	Teschner-Olds	Schmitt, Hall, McCreary	E
Prepare the Way to Zion	Luvaas	Ditson	M

Good Friday

Who Crucified My Lord?	Belcher	Schmitt, Hall, McCreary	M
O Holy Jesu	Lvoff-Grant	G. Schirmer	M

Easter and Sundays Following

Easter Bells Are Ringing	Elmore	Galaxy	D
In Joseph's Lovely Garden	Dickenson	Gray	E
Jesus Christ Is Risen Today	Rowley	Gray	D
Now Let the Heavens Be Joyful	arr. Halter	Schmitt, Hall, McCreary	M
Jesus Lives	Thiman	Gray	M

Ascension and Sundays Following

The Lord Is Exalted	West	Gray	E
All Hail the Power	V. Williams	Oxford	M
With a Voice of Singing	Shaw	G. Schirmer	M

Call to Service

Go Labor On	Gibbons-Clokey	FitzSimons	E

How Lovely Are the Messengers	Mendelssohn	Ditson	D
Rise Up, O Men of God	Miles	FitzSimons	M
Go, Heralds of Salvation	Wilson	Hope	D

Pentecost

With Other Tongues	Palestrina	Boosey and Hawkes	M

Trinity and the Work of the Holy Spirit

Firmly I Believe and Truly	Tomblings	Summy-Birchard	E
Spirit of God	Weaver	Galaxy	M
Come, Thou Holy Spirit	Tschesnokoff-Tkach	Kjos	D
Create in Me a Clean Heart	Mueller	G. Schirmer	E

Mother's Day

A Mother's Day Prayer	Thompson	Summy-Birchard	M

Good Shepherd

Good Shepherd of the Children	Hokanson	Kjos	E
The Lord Is My Shepherd	arr. Black	FitzSimons	E
Shepherd of Tender Youth	Darst	Summy-Birchard	M
The King of Love My Shepherd Is	Shelley	G. Schirmer	M

The Church

Thy Church, O God	Thiman	Novello	M

Redemption Message

I Will Sing of My Redeemer	Thiman	Novello	E
I Lay My Sins on Jesus	Smart	Hope	E
Seek Ye the Lord	Roberts	G. Schirmer	E
God's Son Has Made Me Free	Grieg-Overby	Augsburg	D
Jesus Is My Heart's Delight	Ahle-Bach	Concordia	M

Second Coming of Christ

Lost in the Night	Christiansen	Augsburg	D
When He Shall Come	arr. Hustad	Hope	D
The Trumpet Shall Sound	Scott-Kreisler	Flammer	M

Heaven

In Heaven Above	arr. Christiansen	Augsburg	M
How Lovely Is Thy Dwelling Place	Brahms	Gray	D

Judgment

Turn Back, O Man	Holst	Galaxy	D

Patriotic

God of the Nations	Bourgeois-Strohm	Schmitt, Hall, McCreary	M

Collections of Music Suitable for Church Orchestras or Bands

Title	Publisher
Cathedral Band Book	Kjos
Choice Chorales and Hymns for Band	Concordia
Christmas Carols (arranged by G. E. Holmes)	Rubank
Church Orchestra, The (Vol. 1, 2, 3)	Lorenz
Ensemble Music for Church and School	Hope
Favorite Hymns Collection No. 1	Boosey-Hawkes
Fox Sacred Orchestra Folio (Vol. 1, 2, 3)	Fox
Gospel Hour, The	Schmitt
Hymns of All Churches	Hal Leonard
Sacred Ensemble Band Book	Hansen
Sixteen Chorales by J. S. Bach	G. Schirmer
Sunday Music	Ditson
Symphonic Series of Sacred Song	Rodeheaver
Thirty-five Famous Chorales	Kjos

Music Suitable for Weddings

Hymns for Congregation, Vocal Solo, Choir, or Quartet:

Title	Author-Composer	Tune
God Is Love, His Mercy Brightens	Bowring-Beethoven	Dulcetta
Joyful, Joyful, We Adore Thee	Van Dyke-Beethoven	Hymn to Joy
Love Divine, All Loves Excelling	Wesley-Zundel	Beecher
Now Thank We All Our God	Rinkart-Cruger	Nun Danket
O Perfect Love, All Human Thoughts Transcending	Gurney-Barnby	Sandringham
The King of Love My Shepherd Is	Baker-Dykes	Dominus Regit Me
The Lord's My Shepherd, I'll Not Want	Scottish Psalter-Havergal	Evan

Vocal Solos, Sacred:

Title	Composer	Publisher
A Wedding Benediction	Lovelace	G. Schirmer
Brother James' Air	Jacob	Oxford
Entreat Me Not to Leave Thee	Gounod	G. Schirmer
I Will Sing New Songs of Gladness	Dvorak	Associated
Jesu, Joy of Man's Desiring	Bach	E. C. Schirmer
Jesus, Stand Beside Them	Lovelace	Abingdon
Love Never Faileth	Root	Summy
My Heart Ever Faithful	Bach	G. Schirmer
O Perfect Love	Clokey	J. Fischer
O Perfect Love	Sowerby	Gray

The God of Love My Shepherd Is	Thiman	Gray
The King of Love My Shepherd Is	Shelley	G. Schirmer
The Lord's Prayer	Mallotte	G. Schirmer
Wedding Hymn (from Ptolemy)	Handel	BMI, Canada
Wedding Song	Schuetz	Chantry

Vocal Solos, Secular (for use at reception or bridal shower):

Title	Composer	Publisher
Because	d'Hardelot	Chappell
Calm as the Night	Bohm	G. Schirmer
Dedication	Franz	Ditson
If Thou Be Near	Bach	Witmark
I Love Thee	Grieg	G. Schirmer
I'll Walk Beside You	Murray	Chappell
Through the Years	Youmans	Miller

Collections of Organ Pieces:

Title	Composer or Editor	Publisher
Ceremonial Music for Organ	Purcell-Biggs	Mercury
Easy Service Music for Organ	Franck-Robinson	Hope
Eleven Chorale Preludes	Brahms	Mercury
Four Wedding Marches	Bloch	G. Schirmer
Ninety-three Short Solos for the Hammond Organ		G. Schirmer
Standard Organ Pieces		Appleton-Century-Crofts
Three Short Pieces	Wesley	Gray
Water Music	Handel	J. Fischer
Wedding Music, Vol. 1, 2		Concordia
Wedding Music for the Church Organist and Soloist		Abingdon

Music Suitable for Funerals and Memorial Services

Hymns for Congregation, Vocal Solo, Choir, or Quartet:

Title	Author-Composer	Tune
Abide with Me	Lyte-Monk	Eventide
For All the Saints	How-Vaughan Williams	Sine Nomine
Jerusalem, the Golden	Cluny-Ewing	Ewing
Lead, Kindly Light	Newman-Dykes	Lux Benigna
My Jesus, as Thou Wilt	Schmolk-Von Weber	Jewett
Peace, Perfect Peace	Bickersteth-Caldbeck	Pax Tecum

Ten Thousand Times Ten Thousand	Alford-Dykes	Alford
The Sands of Time Are Sinking	Cousin-Urhan	Rutherford

Vocal Solos:

Title	Composer	Publisher
But the Lord Is Mindful of His Own	Mendelssohn	Novello
Come, Ye Blessed	Scott	G. Schirmer
God Is My Shepherd	Dvorak	Associated
God, My Shepherd, Walks Beside Me	Bach	Gray
I Know That My Redeemer Liveth	Handel	G. Schirmer
I Sought the Lord	Stevenson	G. Schirmer
O God, Our Help in Ages Past	West	A. Schmitt
O Rest in the Lord	Mendelssohn	G. Schirmer
Thou Wilt Keep Him in Perfect Peace	Thiman	Gray

Organ Music:

The organist may effectively use much of the accepted literature for church organ, especially pieces which are of a quiet, reflective nature. He must, however, avoid those which are excessively dramatic, or which tend to display virtuosity or sentimentality.

INDEX